Treatise on Astral Projection, OBE & Lucid Dreaming

Treatise on Astral Projection, OBE & Lucid Dreaming

Himani Vashishta

UNICORN BOOKS

Publisher
UNICORN BOOKS
F-2/16, Ansari Road, Daryaganj, New Delhi-110002
E-mail: info@unicornbooks.in • Website: www.unicornbooks.in
☎ 011-23275434, 23262683, 23250704

Branch : Mumbai
23-25, Zaoba Wadi, Thakurdwar, Mumbai-401002
☎ 022-22010941, 022-22053387
E-mail: rapidex@bom5.vsnl.net.in

ISBN: 978-81-7806-332-4
Treatise on Astral Projection, OBE & Lucid Dreaming

Edition: 2021-22

Printed at : *Param Offsetters, Okhla, New Delhi-110020*

Dedication

To my cute little angel, my nephew Kushagra,
Whose innocent smile always fills my heart with unending joy and whose shining eyes compel me to see the beauty and goodness in this world.

Acknowledgements

I would like to thank all my family members who tolerated all my whims and extraordinary activities since my childhood and yet always gave me their emotional and complete support. Their belief in me made this book possible.

Author's Note

A few years ago, I chanced upon an entirely strange concept. I learnt it was a phenomenon called Astral Projection and Out of Body Experience (OBE). I can claim that even during my childhood, I had some ability of lucid dreaming. I can very well remember that even at a tender age I had seen hundreds of dreams that proved true in my real life. Those real dreams confirmed my faith in the concept of Astral Projection.

Astral Projection or Out-of-body experience is a process through which our consciousness can leave our physical body and travel anywhere, free and unrestricted by our normal physical boundaries. I can understand any average person may perhaps reject the notion of Astral Projection. It is my sincere request to my readers to read this book with an open heart and mind and try to verify its reality themselves.

This handbook is the result of my five years of extensive research, study and personal practice of the Astral Projection phenomenon.

As a beginner, the many obstacles and problems that I had faced, I have tried to project here through this book to pre-warn my future practitioners.

This handbook is with a completely pragmatic approach, not prescribed for light reading as it contains no speculations or stories, and rather contains only dry, hard facts.

My introduction to this enticing subject came when one day I had an unconscious Out-of-body experience. I was confused. Was it a dream? But after searching on Internet I found so many references of people who shared similar experiences. I then determinedly decided to learn conscious OBE.

I read so many books on this subject but most of the authors left me dissatisfied. Some books provided a deep philosophical theory on Astral Projection but lacked practical use. Books having some practical applications lacked logical theory. Some books to my disappointment contained case study after case study, and a series of good and intriguing stories about Astral Projection.

I longed for more!

As an author, finally, after indepth evaluation of this concept, I decided to write on this topic in a very simple language and with user-friendly approach.

This guidebook has the potential to let anyone, regardless of spiritual or metaphysical training, achieve a conscious Out-of-body experience and avail its benefits.

This book is in easy-to-understand and well-illustrated format.

Being an astral practitioner myself I believe that there is nothing impossible about this phenomenon if tried correctly with right effort and with frequent practice.

Avoiding too many technicalities, through this book I have tried to give as much information as possible, both theoretical and practical.

Astral Projection is just one of the many applications that help us know why we are here in the first place. So, I sincerely feel we all should learn this amazing theory and art and give a positive direction to our lives.

I request my readers to treat this book like a clean slate and judge it by one's own experiments and practical experiences.

I hope this book will prove to be a life-changing experience for my readers.

Best wishes for Astral Travel!

—Himani Vashishta

Author Introduction

Himani Vashishta is a Poet-turned-Author.

Her first poem was published in the book *"Blossom Of India"* through a poetry competition held by an American Poetry Society, *"Poet of Mars"*. But Himani is known for her Fantasy novel *"Princess Of Falcons"* which brought her huge applause. She writes fluently in both, English and Hindi languages. Recently, her Hindi essay *'Dukh'* has been published in the book *'Anand'* and two more Poetry books *'Garden Of Love'* and *'Let Him Play The Music Again'* are published online.

Born in (Bikaner) Rajasthan on 12th December, Himani was brought up in Haryana. Himani Vashishta has done MBA & LLB. She comes from an Indian family that takes pride in being part of a rich cultural heritage and traditions, now entwined with modern-day living. She is a descendent of a long line of ancestors who have been appreciated mainly for their scholastic attributes.

From a very tender age, Himani felt inclined to write poetry and short stories. Her passion for fantasies further developed a flair for writing fiction.

The author is a keen lover of art, won several prizes in painting, cartooning and acting. She has varied interests ranging from gardening, origami, occult sciences and astrology to blogging, etc.

The writer loves to get feedback from her readers. She can be contacted at: *himani.vashishta6@gmail.com.*

Author Introduction

Contents

1. **General Background and Introduction 23**
   What is Astral Projection? 23
   Historical, Cultural and Religious Background of Astral Projection 24
   Cultural Background 24
      Ancient Egypt *24*
      Ancient Greece 24
      China 25
      India 25
      Japan 25
      Amazon 25
   Religious Background 26
      Hindu Philosophy 26
      Western Philosophies 26
      Bible 26
      Islam 27
   Notable Practitioners 27
   Difference Between Astral Projection and OBE ... 28
2. **Benefits of Astral Projection......................... 29**
   1. Definite belief in afterlife (i.e., Immortality) 29
   2. Understanding our purpose of existence 29
   3. Inculcates wisdom and knowledge enhancement 30
   4. Enhances personal development 30
   5. An inner calmness 31
   6. Healing 31
   7. Fun of flying 31

8. Meeting Guides and Enlightened Spirits 31
9. Overall Well-being and Personal
Development 32
10. Boost Psychic Abilities 32
11. Increased Respect for Life and Reduction
in Hostility 32
12. Experience Tranquillity 33
13. Meet Deceased Loved Ones or Say
Better Farewell 33
14. Seeking the Answers 33
15. Understanding the Meaning of Life 34
16. Spiritual Growth and Spiritual Strength 34
17. Increases Passion for Life 34
18. Increased Intuition 34
19. Know Other Realities 35
20. Exploring Old Cultures and History 35
21. Energy Healing 35
22. Discover New Worlds 35
23. Meeting and Seeing Distant Friends 35
24. Exploring Earth 36
25. Enhances Memory and Intelligence 36
26. Broader Perspective 36
27. Reviewing Past Moments 36
28. Helping Spirits 37
29. Seeing is Believing 37
30. Escaping Routine Life 37
31. Discovering Aliens 37
32. Going to Inaccessible Places without Limits
and Fear 37
33. Increased Self-responsibility and Compassion 38

34. Better Sleep 38
35. Adventure 38
36. Creative Inspiration 38
37. Communicating With Nature 38
38. Surpassing Physical Limitations 39
39. Experiencing Immortality 39
40. Travelling to the Past or Future 39
41. Self-knowledge 39
42. Confirming Physics Theories, Scientific Facts and Learn about Dimensional Structure 39
43. Accessing New Senses 40
44. Sense of Freedom 40
45. Living out Fantasies 40

3. Preparing For Astral Projection 41

Starting Out 41

1. Relaxing Physically 42

Physical Relaxation Exercises: 42

Regressive Relaxation 43

2. Mental Relaxation Exercises 44

Concentration Exercises 45

Energy Breathing 45

Spot Stare: 45

The Trance State 46

4. Astral Projection Techniques 47

Projection Techniques 48

1. Rope Technique 48

2. Anchor Technique 50

3. Muldoon's Thirst Technique 51

4. Lift/Roll Out Technique 52

5. Object Technique 53

6. Affirmations Technique 53
7. Red Spot Technique 54
8. Stretch-out Technique 54
9. Trampoline Technique 55
10. Astral Projection from Lucid Dreams 56
5. Astral Planes & Astral World 57
Astral Plane 57
Planes of Existence 58
First Plane 58
Second Plane 58
Third Plane 59
Fourth Plane 59
Fifth Plane 59
Sixth Plane 59
Seventh Plane 59
Astral World & Astral Entities 60
Human Entities 60
Non-human Entities 61
Artificial Entities 61
6. Pre-Projection Phenomena 63
Some Common Pre-Projection Sensations 63
1. Vibrations 63
2. Sleep Paralysis 64
3. Buzzing and Other Sounds 65
4. Hallucinations 65
5. Sensing a Presence 66
6. Weight Changes 66
7. Temperature Changes 67
8. Movement Sensations 67
9. Rapid Heart Rate 67

10. Breathing Changes 67
11. Eye Movements 68
12. Blackout 68
13. Waking Paralysis 68
14. Heavy Exit Sensations 68
15. Lost Focus During the Exit 69
7. Post-Projection Basics **70**
1. Silver Cord 70
2. Control Your Thoughts 71
3. Communication During Astral Projection 71
4. Movement on the Astral Plane 71
5. Astral Vision 72
6. Astral Blindness 72
7. Duality 73
8. Nourishment and Clothing during Astral Projection 73
9. Returning Back to Physical Body 74
8. Related Concepts **75**
1. Third Eye 75
2. Etheric Matter 76
3. Doppelganger Phenomena 76
4. Remote Viewing 76
5. Near Death Experience (NDE) 77
6. Spontaneous Projection 77
7. Lucid Dreaming 77
8. Dreamwalking 78
9. Akashic Records 78
10. Death 78
11. REM (Rapid Eye Movement) 79
12. Spirits 79

13. Calling For Help 80
14. Developing Clairvoyance 80
15. The Aura 81
Colors of the Aura and their Nature 81
16. Affirmations 83
9. Lucid Dreaming 84
What is Lucid Dreaming? 84
The Benefits of Lucid Dreaming 85
1. Overcoming Nightmares 85
2. Wish Fulfilment 86
3. Emotional Benefits 86
4. Adventure and Fantasy 86
5. Ahead of Entertainment 87
6. Rehearsal 87
7. Transcendence 87
8. Healing 87
9. Problem Solving and Creativity 88
Prerequisites for Lucid Dreaming 88
Steps of Lucid Dreaming 89
1. Mental Preparation 89
2. Dream Recall 89
3. Dreams Understanding 92
4. Dream Awareness 93
Lucid Dreaming Tips 93
Lucid Dreaming FAQs 94
10. Common Mistakes and Problems & Astral Projection Tips 98
1. Attempting at Night-time 98
2. Fear 99
Overcoming Fear 100

3. Eagerness & Impatience 101
4. Inner Thoughts & Dialogue 101
5. Misunderstanding Body Asleep
vs. Relaxation 102
6. The Visualization Problem 102
7. Remembering the Projection 103
8. Paralysis, after an apparently Successful
Projection 104
Astral Projection Tips 105
1. Overcoming Fear 105
2. Practice Environment 105
3. Practise Regularly 106
4. Approach to Literature 106
5. Use an External Aid 107
6. Remain Firmly Determined
& Persistent 107
7. Proper Meditation 107
8. Manage Our Physical World 107
9. Be Aware & Open 108
10. Communicating with Like-Minded People
or Other Practitioners 108
11. Personal Analysis 108
12. Pen down Experiences 108
13. Miscellaneous Tips 109
11. Frequently Asked Questions (FAQs).......... 112

Chapter 1

General Background and Introduction

What is Astral Projection?

Astral Projection is the act of consciously separating spirit from physical body and letting the spirit travel anywhere without body and returning with full memory. This is an occult skill through which our soul can leave our body with full awareness and can travel anywhere, any city, any country, or say, through time and space.

Astral Projection or Out-of-body experience is a process through which our consciousness leaves our physical body and is free to travel anywhere, unrestricted by our normal physical boundaries. When you astral project, what you are actually doing is shifting your consciousness from your physical body to your astral body.

We all unconsciously travel outside our bodies every night when we are asleep. But with the right guidance and practice, we can train ourselves to achieve this with 100% consciousness and awareness.

When we are born on this physical plane, we all come with a specific purpose. That purpose may be different for different people. But as we grow older, we forget why we are here. So, we wander aimlessly and often end up wasting our lives.

Astral Projection is one way to help us know why we are here in the first place. So, I sincerely feel we all should learn this amazing art and give a positive direction to our lives.

Historical, Cultural and Religious Background of Astral Projection

Throughout the history of different cultures, civilizations, countries and religions, there are various documentations of Astral Projections.

These relations give us an idea of the universal character of this capacity of leaving the body.

Cultural Background

Ancient Egypt

Ancient Egyptians believed that the soul has the ability to hover outside the physical body. The Egyptian priests called their astral body as Kha and they left behind various inscriptions and diagrams on the walls of several temples, showing something subtle and glow of light leaving the physical body.

Ancient Greece

Some Greek philosophers like Plato, Herodotus, Plutarch mentioned references of such instances and Temple of Eleusis.

In a story by Plutarch, there was a very bad, dishonest man, Arisdeu in the first century. One day, accidentally, he fell and his head hit against a rock, throwing him in coma for a couple of days. Arisdeu that time had a Near death experience (NDE). When he was out of his body, a spiritual guide talked to him and, on the other dimension, he examined certain things.

When he woke up in his body, his relatives were going to bury him. Since that experience, Arisdeu transformed himself and changed his ethics, behaviour and became a good citizen.

China

The alchemical practice of Taoists involves drawing energy, circulating and creation of an energy body by meditational breathing. Their legends depict various instances of leaving of body by the spirit. Many Chino-Tibetan meditation methods are derived from Buddhist channels. Lord Buddha is said to have achieved the heights in Astral Projection.

India

Yogic tradition of India presents a very detailed system of meditation and astral projection. Astral projection is considered as a Siddhi, achievable by yoga practitioners through meditation technics and practice.

Japan

In Japanese mythology, an Ikiry is a manifestation of the spirit of a living person separating from the body.

Amazon

They believed in 'soul flight' which has various benefits like healing. The soul's flight to the sky was known to consult spiritual guides.

Religious Background

Hindu Philosophy

In ancient Hindu scriptures like Yoga Vashishta-Maharamayana, there is mention about Astral Experiences. Modern notable Indian Astral Practitioners are Ramakrishna Paramahansa Sri Yogananda, Avatar Meher Baba and Osho Bhagwan Shree Rajneesh.

Western Philosophies

There are varied Western theories in this regard, like Classical, Medieval, Renaissance Hermeticism, Neoplatonism, and later, Theosophist and Rosicrucian.

They believed that the astral body is linked to the physical body by an intermediate source of light.

Bible

Bible has several evidences of cases of conscious projections such as in Ezequiel, III:14; Apocalypse of Juan, 1:10 and 11; 4:2; as well as in Epistles of Pablo of Tarsus (II Corynthios, 12:2).

Some citations of Bible mentions Astral Projection.

Our Astral body is attached to the physical body by means of a silver cord. The final chapter of the Biblical Book of Ecclesiastes is often cited in this respect: "Before the silver cord be loosed, or the golden bowl be broken, or the pitcher be shattered at the fountain, or the wheel be broken at the cistern."

Paul's statement "I know a man in Christ, fourteen years ago, (whether in the body I know not, or out of the body I know not, God knows) such a one caught up to the third heaven..." is most often referred to the astral planes.

Islam

The holy book of Muslims-Quran, describes an out of body journey, in which apostle Muhammad without his body visits Jerusalem and onward to seven heavens.

Notable Practitioners

- The first practitioner to write extensively on this topic is Emanuel Swedenborg. He wrote about out-of-body experiences in his Spiritual Diary (1747-65).
- A fictional work "Louis Lambert" by a French philosopher and novelist Honoré de Balzac's gave hint about his astral experiences.
- In the twentieth century, many books were published by Astral practitioners but the most famous practitioners and authors are Robert Monroe, Robert Bruce, Oliver Fox, William Buhlman, Sylvan Muldoon and Hereward Carrington.
- Robert Monroe popularized the term "OBE" and his books have been translated into a large number of languages. He also started a research institute for OBE.
- Waldo Vieira, a physician and a notable Astral Practitioner claimed to have astral projections from the age of 9 years and he wrote numerous articles and more than 20 books.
- The President of and a researcher at International Academy of Consciousness, Wagner Alegretti, also a notable Astral projector, was featured on the Discovery Channel.

- Carrington and Muldoon, both notable practitioners and psychical researchers, jointly published a book, 'The Projection of the Astral Body' in 1929.

Difference Between Astral Projection and OBE

I have noticed that most of the authors and people use these two terms interchangeably but there is a slight difference between these two terms.

These concepts can be differentiated on the amount of control. For Astral Projection, it takes a great amount of concentration, dedication and practice, whereas an OBE tends to be less controlled and less rewarding.

Astral Projection normally occurs consciously by achieving relaxation and meditation, an out-of-body experience has been known to happen at virtually any time. On the other hand, astral projection is a lot more controlled.

Occurrence of OBE is known to have something to do with a physical or emotional shock to the system like during grave illness, accident, high medication.

Overall we can say that Astral Projection is a much more enlightening and rewarding experience than OBE.

♦♦♦

Chapter 2

Benefits of Astral Projection

1. Definite belief in afterlife (i.e., Immortality)

Somewhere we all have fear of death in our hearts. Yet every one of us is aware that the soul is immortal. We know that our physical body perishes but not the soul. However, once we achieve the first-hand experience of astral projection, then our belief is confirmed. Anyone who has experienced astral projection, knows that our existence beyond the physical body is possible; our consciousness can exist outside our body. This belief overcomes fear of death completely. Astral projection lets us investigate if there really is an afterlife waiting after death, which gives us so much confidence and certainty in this life. After the confirmation of afterlife, death may become a less frightening experience and even an amazing, spiritual adventure, something to be accepted without fear and hesitation when the time arrives.

2. Understanding our purpose of existence

An experienced astral projector starts getting glimpses of his past life and begins to understand himself better.

Astral Projection enhances self-awareness, increases our level of understanding, and deepens or accelerates our spiritual knowledge. The knowledge we can't acquire in our everyday life can be acquired through astral projection. It helps in learning about ourselves, about earth or, say, about the whole universe. It inculcates a sense of universalism, the feeling of which is breathtaking,... exhilarating. The recollections of past lives and incidents aid in finding our purpose of existence. The disclosure of past life can make it less complicated to solve the problems of the present. We can even overcome certain traumas and stress.

3. Inculcates wisdom and knowledge enhancement

We can meet advanced enlightened beings, and guides even from distant ancient traditions, and can learn from them the mysteries of life and death. Out-of-body experiences have the unique ability to provide first hand information and wisdom far beyond the limits of our physical perceptions, which can't be imposed upon by other basic teachings and beliefs.

4. Enhances personal development

The revelation that we are more than just physical beings, gives us firm belief that we are capable of much more than previously imagined.

Once we consciously control our non-physical self, we can unlock the unlimited knowledge of our subconscious and harness our ability to explore the universe. The entire subject of human potential is dramatically expanded beyond all current concepts and comprehension.

5. An inner calmness

Many report feeling at peace with themselves and with others as well. They develop an inner tranquillity that is hard to describe.

6. Healing

Astral Projection raises energy levels so that more powerful etheric energy may be utilised for physical and mental healing. The astral projector can heal himself and others mentally and physically with the knowledge and control and learn to utilize energy acquired through out-of-body experiences.

7. Fun of flying

The most happy and simple activity in the astral projection is flying. We can feel the joy of flying anywhere and at the speed we desire, only through Astral Projection. During Astral Projection, even the sky is NOT the limit. Like birds we can fly, like balloons we can float in the air and move through a city, can fly over beautiful landscapes, or even glide through outer space. We can jump from a building or a mountain or swim like a fish. We can fly to any city or can go and see our departed souls.

8. Meeting Guides and Enlightened Spirits

During Astral Projection it is possible to meet your Spiritual Guide who can be a source of inspiration and spiritual knowledge and help us advance spiritually. We can feel their positive energy and converse with them on deeper, inner levels. But we should never invite unknown spirits.

9. Overall Well-being and Personal Development

Astral Projection increases enlightened perspective of our current existence and purpose. This broader perspective is instrumental in awakening new levels of personal intellectual growth.

Astral Projection helps in becoming better in all spheres of life – intensifying of intellectual capacities, expansion of self-awareness, overall well-being, increase in self-confidence, stronger memory recall, control of stress and anger and exercise emotional balance. We can learn to manage and control our own energies. Out-of-body experiences help us to break free from old mental ruts and bad habits.

10. Boost Psychic Abilities

Astral Projection increases spirituality and paranormal experiences by opening the unused areas of our mind. Regular out-of-body experiences boost psychic abilities, such as telepathy, clairvoyance, precognition, intuition, foretelling, ability to see auras and many other psychic abilities.

11. Increased Respect for Life and Reduction in Hostility

Out-of-body experiences inculcates feeling of universalism, helps understanding life in a better way and gives an inner tranquillity. It removes petty jealousy, hostile feelings and improves relations with fellow beings. This is because the astral projector starts seeing life from a very broad perspective. He realizes that he is more than just his physical body and the consciousness continues after death. Astral Projectors begin to hate violence and killing.

12. Experience Tranquillity

Astral Projection increases spirituality. Astral Projectors usually feel at peace with themselves and others. They develop an inner serenity and satisfaction.

13. Meet Deceased Loved Ones or Say Better Farewell

Death of our loved ones is the saddest experience in our life. It breaks us from inside. Probably, we could establish contact with the spirit of our known departed souls, if they exist on the same astral plane. We could request their spirit to connect with us. We could concentrate on meeting them during Astral Projection by calling their names. We can seek them out in the Astral Sphere and reunite with them to feel the warmth of their presence. These meetings could prove very helpful because we can request for their guidance and healing.

14. Seeking the Answers

Since childhood, we have so many queries in our minds, such questions which can't be answered by our parents or even teachers, like – Who am I? What is my purpose? What should I do? What happens after death?

Sometimes, we face some very heartbreaking incident in our life, when we begin to contemplate why it had to happen to me, when I was not at any fault? The answer may lie in our past lives. The same situation I had faced a few years back. The knowledge of my past life through

Astral Projection helped me to understand my present situation and helped me to accept my pain more readily. Thus, out-of-body exploration provides a powerful method for all of us to obtain the answers we seek.

15. Understanding the Meaning of Life

As a seeker of truth, Astral Projection can be exercised to discover the truth about life and the meaning behind it, and its purpose. Many ancient and modern sages, mystics and scientists have used it.

16. Spiritual Growth and Spiritual Strength

Astral learning helps in spiritual progression. Since ages, Astral Projection has been used by mystics and sages for spiritual growth. Astral Projection confirms our belief in immortality and gives us insights into our spiritual nature. Instead of viewing ourselves as physical beings possessing a soul, we start to recognize ourselves as the soul temporarily possessing a physical body. This inculcates a feeling of universalism and removes fear, hostility and materialism. We start to learn the purpose of our life and existence.

17. Increases Passion for Life

Out-of-body experience is an extraordinary experience. It fills adventure and excitement in our life. Everyday it gives an opportunity to experience a new adventure.

18. Increased Intuition

Astral Projection definitely increases intuitive powers. Subliminal connections to the mind are stronger and can become easier to recognise. It helps in tapping unused areas of our mind and intellect, thus enhancing mental abilities.

19. Know Other Realities

Astral experience permits us to witness other realities, or scope, beyond the physical plane. We can see the place where we lived before entering into this present birth, and we can also go to the place where we will go after the physical death. So, many mysteries can be solved. The Astral Projection is a goldmine for anyone with interests in psychology and human behaviour.

20. Exploring Old Cultures and History

In the astral world, nothing is time bound. One can go back in time to explore the ancient cultures throughout history, or meet people from that era or can even meet any historical figure.

21. Energy Healing

In the physical world, we are often surrounded by negative energy where we feel dull and lethargic. The energy gained and generated through astral experience can be used to heal our physical body.

22. Discover New Worlds

Advanced and experienced astral projectors can travel to distant worlds in space, discover new forms of life and can explore some exotic new territories.

23. Meeting and Seeing Distant Friends

Our physical limitations sometimes prevent us from meeting our dearest friend. But through Astral Projection we can meet our friend, visit his place and see what our friend or relative is doing. Astral meeting can be much more rewarding and connecting and could improve the relationship in the physical world.

24. Exploring Earth

Every one of us likes to travel and visit new places but time, money and governmental policies set heavy obstacles here on Earth, whereas in the Astral Sphere, there is no place we cannot go to. Just by naming and our will, we can visit the highest mountain, the steepest valley, the thickest forest and the deepest ocean.

25. Enhances Memory and Intelligence

Astral Projection stimulates areas of the brain previously untapped during normal physical life. Astral experiences increase memory recall, awareness and intelligence.

26. Broader Perspective

The knowledge gained by astral experiences helps to understand the situation better. The projector begins to see things and life from an insightful new perspective that was never existent because of the limitations of the physical world. The insightful new perspective positively helps in solving frustrating physical problems with a new approach.

27. Reviewing Past Moments

We all have had some beautiful moments in our past and we often desire to live them again. An Astral Projection is not time bound. We can gain access to our old memories and re-live or see them from a new perspective. Even from the perspective of the other entity in that old memory.

28. Helping Spirits

Experienced projectors can help those spirits who get stuck in certain places for some reason, and they need a bit of a push to help them to get unstuck. Sometimes, spirits of our loved ones may be in need of our help.

29. Seeing is Believing

From our childhood, we are listening that, in our body, our soul resides and that soul is immortal. Several religions, spiritual authors and philosophers can talk endlessly about theories and beliefs, but when we really experience it, then only this theory confirms.

30. Escaping Routine Life

Astral Projection brings a new excitement in our routine life. Astral projection can really enrich a person's life and bring a new quality to it.

31. Discovering Aliens

We all have heard about aliens but rarely anyone of us has seen them. Astral Projection may provide us the ability and a great tool to find aliens.

32. Going to Inaccessible Places without Limits and Fear

Our Astral bodies are indestructible. So, without any harm in Astral Projection, we can go to such places where we can't reach with our physical bodies like –

Inside the Earth core, deep under the ocean, Visit to Sun, Moon and other planets.

33. Increased Self-responsibility and Compassion

Astral Projection is an eye opening experience. Those who experience it, have the first hand knowledge about life; they learn that they themselves are the creators of their physical life. They feel they are completely responsible for all their deeds and activities.

34. Better Sleep

Those who face sleeping disorders, have reported improvement because conscious projection of the astral body draws more energy and tranquillity.

35. Adventure

Astral Projection is usually adopted by those who love adventures. Travelling to unknown distances and experiencing new and exciting things is quite adventurous.

36. Creative Inspiration

As a writer and a painter, I can say that the experiences of Astral Projection give endless material for inspiration. The feelings, sights and amazing experiences in the Astral world can inspire us in whatever we do. In the Astral world, we have access to deeper insight and connection, so our work of art can become more amazing and beautiful.

37. Communicating With Nature

Astral Projection connects us with nature. The amazing scenery, we couldn't even imagine, visually makes us talk to nature.

38. Surpassing Physical Limitations

In Astral realm, physically disabled persons can bypass their limitations, even a deaf person can hear and a blind person may see, a handicapped person may walk or fly.

39. Experiencing Immortality

Immortality is just a dream here on Earth, but in the Astral world, it's a reality of life. There is no time or physical boundation.

40. Travelling to the Past or Future

Time is very fluid in the Astral world. So it is possible to travel back in past, go back to different historical eras or one can view future events too.

41. Self-knowledge

The Astral world is the ideal place to learn many details about our self. We can visit our past lives, talk to people who have known us for centuries, and even contact other parts of our self for deeper knowledge.

42. Confirming Physics Theories, Scientific Facts and Learn about Dimensional Structure

Science is full of theories and suppositions, but due to physical limitations, we can't experiment all those theories. Through Astral Projection tools, we can use all of our extra-dimensional senses to get insight and true knowledge into anything, physical or metaphysical. We can directly experiment with the dimensional structure and learn about space and time.

43. Accessing New Senses

In Astral realm, we have extra senses and 360-degree vision. Astral Projection naturally activates psychic powers, remote viewing, clairvoyance, telepathy, intuition and more.

44. Sense of Freedom

"We are born free but everywhere we are in ties" the classical quotation by Roussou is true regarding our physical life on earth. But out-of-body experiences give us a strong sense of freedom and lack of limitations. Out-of-body experiences remind us that behind this world of delusion, we are really a free and cheerful spirit.

45. Living out Fantasies

The Astral plane has such incredibly, indescribable beauty that it is beyond imagination. There we can create fully interactive 3D fantasies, craft our own fantasy scenery.

What are you waiting for, go and create your fantasy world now!

♦♦♦

Chapter 3

Preparing For Astral Projection

Astral Projection is for everyone, irrespective of age, gender, religion, but the basic requirement for a successful projection is high concentration power and a strong will and commitment to project.

Starting Out

There are some general requirements to be fulfilled before starting Astral Projection. These conditions are not strictly required to be followed but they are minimum optimum requirements for successful Astral Projection:

1. One can choose any position in which he is most comfortable. Like sitting in a comfortable chair or lying down.

2. The practising room should be quiet with comfortable temperature and free from any distracting background noise.

3. Soft and dim light in the room is advised. Beginners should avoid projecting in complete darkness, as the fear of the dark and unknown may stop them. This may hamper your progress.

4. Fried food, meat, alcoholic drinks should be avoided. One should not try to project under intoxication.

5. To breathe freely, have loose clothing and remove any jewellery and watch is recommended.

6. To avoid unwanted distractions during your Projection before practice, one should go to the bathroom and empty the bladder.

7. During projection, body may lose heat. So one may cover himself with a blanket.

8. Keep tensions and disturbing thoughts away from you. Keep them aside in an imaginary box. Still if you can't stop thinking too much and get relaxed then try some other day.

There are two major requirements to trigger Astral Projection:

1. Relaxing Physically

2. Relaxing Mentally

1. Relaxing Physically

A practitioner's aim should be to reach at a stage where he is not even aware of his physical body. A projector necessarily needs to relax his body 100% while staying awake. Without physical relaxation, it's almost impossible to exit your Astral body consciously.

Physical Relaxation Exercises:

Deep Breathing Exercise

Deep breathing is a great way to relax the body. So, it is used extensively in Yoga and martial arts. This is one of the most popular techniques for whole body relaxation as it gets everything into synchrony.

Deep Breathing Exercise Steps:

1. Settle in your comfortable position.

2. Try to keep your mind empty.

3. Slowly start inhaling through nose and first fill with air the lower part of your chest, then middle and finally top part of your chest and lungs. This procedure must be done slowly for over 8-10 seconds.

4. For a second or two, try to hold your breath and then slowly release the air and relax.

5. With a gap of a few seconds, repeat this procedure but avoid overdoing it as you may feel dizzy, so slow down.

6. For better relaxation, imagine yourself at a very peaceful place like a calm ocean or a very blissful place and try to harmonise with your breathing pattern along with that imagination like feel of the gentle rise and retreat of sea waves with your inhale and exhale.

Regressive Relaxation

Regressive relaxation is beginning to focus each muscle from 'Head to Toe'. Mentally relax that body part and then move down. Likewise, Progressive relaxation can be started by moving from feet to head.

Our aim must be to focus on every part and muscle of body to consciously relax it. For beginners, this process may take up to ten minutes but once we become accustomed to it, this time period may be reduced to one minute.

Regressive Relaxation Exercise Steps:

1. Settle in your comfortable position and close your eyes.

2. Feel your forehead and imagine your mind very relaxed and calm.

3. Feel your eyes. Visualize a very calm and tension-free feeling. Relax your eyes.

4. Feel your face and cheeks. Release every tensed muscle and relax.

5. Feel your mouth and jaw. Unclench your jaw muscles and let them be relaxed absolutely.

6. Feel your neck. Feel it completely relaxed.

7. Feel your hands. Feel their weight and now consciously relax them.

8. Feel your chest and then abdomen. Feel your breathing and slightly make it deeper and deeper.

9. Feel your buttocks. Feel their weight and consider them very relaxed.

10. Feel your thighs. Imagine them very relaxed.

11. Feel your knees. Visualize them very relaxed.

12. Feel your feet. Feel their weight. Now picture them very relaxed.

13. Still if you are not feeling fully relaxed, you can repeat this whole bodily relaxation process.

2. Mental Relaxation Exercises

Mental Relaxation involves concentrating 100% on what we are doing. When we try to concentrate over something or try to keep our mind free, hundreds of thoughts surprisingly occupy our mind, whereas actually, at that time, we are trying to keep our mind focused. Silencing our mind is one of the toughest tasks. We should only try being an observer of those thoughts rather than analyzing them or we can put our worries in an imaginary box for some time.

Sounds of the things happening around us or near us (Like the thought that .... who is on the door?) may prove quite distracting, we must practise to ignore and quash them as it improves concentration level too.

Mental relaxation and concentration are non-negotiable for achieving body separation or Astral Projection.

Concentration Exercises

Energy Breathing

It is a purification exercise. Energy breathing exercise opens our chakras for absorbing positive energy when we inhale and releasing negative energy as we exhale.

Shut your eyes and relax your body and mind. Now start breathing slowly. Your whole concentration must be on breathing. Now imagine the air you are breathing, imagine that the air you are inhaling is bright, colourful and full of positive energy. The air you exhale, imagine that as black, murky and toxic. This way now you are imagining positive energy filling your body when you inhale and negativity leaving you as you exhale.

Spot Stare

Try to empty your mind of all thoughts and force it to blankness. Now choose a spot on a wall and keep gazing at it gently without focusing over it. There shouldn't be any thought in your mind while gazing at the spot. To clear your mind, you can concentrate hard on your breathing. Don't analyze any thought. Rather don't allow it to finish in your mind. Practise this exercise many times a day to achieve better concentration power.

The Trance State

Trance state is the state in which our body enters the sleep state while our conscious mind is fully awake.

Once we achieve a deep level of physical relaxation and mental calmness, we feel that our body has started to get very heavy. This heaviness is the main symptom of reaching the trance state.

♦♦♦

Chapter 4

Astral Projection Techniques

Once body becomes relaxed and mind is calm, in the next step, to trigger Astral Projection, we need an exit technique. There are several ways of achieving Astral Projection. Here I am only describing the most common and the most useful methods that I have come across. Every individual finds a different method more suited to him. So it's simply a case of experimenting until one finds the technique that works best for him. Still there is no single ideal method or entirely effective formula to leave the body.

Different people have individual personalities, physical constitutions and beliefs.

I am illustrating many different kinds of techniques as there is no universal method that works for everyone. Whatever method you choose, you are unlikely to get a result on the very first night, or even on the first few nights. Don't get frustrated when nothing happens at first, as it is a matter of practice. Sometimes, you need to change your technique also or you can mix the attributes of various techniques to meet your personal needs.

Before I discuss Projection Techniques, I would like to strongly recommend not to use any kind of drugs or alcohol to induce Astral Projection. Drugs harm spiritual growth and by using them, you will travel on lower Astral Plane, which is gloomy, fully perplexing and disorienting and filled with negative energy. Thus, use of drugs will rather make your Astral experience unpleasant.

Projection Techniques

1. *Rope Technique*

This method was developed by Robert Bruce. It is one of the easiest techniques around and my exit technique too. This method does not require much visualization.

The crux of this projection technique is an invisible, imaginary ROPE hanging from your ceiling. The use of this ROPE is to exert dynamic pressure at a single point on your astral body which forces its separation from the physical body.

We need to imagine the action of pulling ourselves hand over hand up a rope. This Rope technique exerts a high level of pressure directly on a single point of the astral body by focusing all our thoughts into one strong, vibrant action.

To get the feel of the Rope, stick a length of ribbon, string or rope to the ceiling above you and hang it within your arms' reach so that you can easily touch it. To get used to where it is in your mind, touch it frequently. This rope is only a tactile aid which conditions your mind to where the invisible, imaginary Rope is. When our mind becomes tuned to it, then it becomes easier to imagine our self reaching out and climbing the Rope with imaginary Hands.

We actually do not need to visualize, or see, the Rope at any time, our mind just knows where it is supposed to be. All this method requires is reaching out and climbing on the invisible, imaginary Rope with your imaginary Hands. It exerts a direct pressure on one point of the ethereal body.

Try to imagine the feel of a strong, thick, coarse rope in your hands but don't try to visualize this Rope because visualization wastes valuable mental resources which can be better used to put direct pressure on your astral body. Imagine you are reaching out and climbing this coarse Rope in dark pitch, where you can't see it at all, but you know where the Rope is and you can imagine the feel of it.

Climb on the Rope hand over hand, upwards, and then you will feel a heavy sensation. Due to exerting pressure on your ethereal body, you may enter into the trance state but ignore it and concentrate on what you are doing. By exerting dynamic pressure on the ethereal body you may feel a slight dizzy sensation inside.

As you progress, you will feel the vibrations or feel paralyzed or may hear buzzing sounds but don't stop, concentrate on climbing your rope. These exit sensations are a natural effect of energy flow through all the hundreds of major and minor chakras in your body.

Finally, you will feel yourself free from your body, hovering above your body in the direction of your imaginary rope.

2. *Anchor Technique*

This is a very popular technique. The key ingredient of this method is to focus on an anchor point. There are two kinds of this technique:

- Fixed anchor
- Moving anchor

Fixed Anchor

After attaining trance state, try to focus on any point outside your physical body. You can simply focus on a point in space, or you can focus on any familiar object. When you clearly see the focus point in your mind's eye, try to 'feel' how solid it is, try to push it, pull it, or move it (do all in your mind). The focus point must be absolutely solid and totally fixed. In our mental imagination, we should not be able to move it.

Once you are completely agreed that the focus point is totally fixed, and it can't be moved, then imagine yourself reaching out to the focus point with your arms and grabbing hold of it. Be cautious, anchor should not move. Try to pull the object towards you, at first gently, and then gradually pull it harder and harder. Slowly as you pull it, you will feel yourself moving towards the focus point. Lastly, you will find yourself at the focus point outside your physical body.

Moving Anchor

This technique is used more than 'Fixed Anchor' technique. Still I personally give preference to Fixed Anchor method.

Once you reach the trance state, just imagine an object about six feet away in front of your eyes. You need to make it also a familiar object. When you can see the object clearly in your mind's eye, then feel you are pulling this object at you like a magnet. Slowly, slowly start moving the object towards you and feel the pull of the object on you. Gradually, you will feel the pull getting stronger as you repeat the process 5 or 6 times, moving the object closer each time.

When you become used to the movement of the object, then begin to move the object to and fro like a wave in a fluid motion. Feel this wave on you as the pull gets stronger and weaker and stronger again. At last, when the object virtually reaches you, the strength of the pulling force, combined with that wave-like motion, will exert pressure on your astral body, pulling you out.

3. *Muldoon's Thirst Technique*

This technique is propounded by Sylvan Muldoon. Yet this is a very effective technique for Projection but this is not featured in pleasant methods.

Because this technique requires increasing thirst by every means we can, in this technique, we must refrain from drinking for some hours before going to bed.

Before sleeping, keep a glass of water in front of you and stare into it and imagine drinking, but don't drink. Eat a pinch or two of salt and keep the glass of water at some convenient place away from your bed and then rehearse in your mind all the actions necessary to get the glass of water... like getting up, reaching out for the glass, and so on. When you go to bed, just think about your thirst and the means of quenching it. During the night, you might rouse in your dream and find your astral body walking towards the glass of water.

4. *Lift/Roll Out Technique*

Perhaps this is the most popular projection technique. A deep level of relaxation and visualization is required for this projection technique. After attaining trance state, you need to use your powers of visualization. You simply need to imagine yourself floating upwards out of your body. Use affirmations and tell yourself all the time how pleasant it is to do this, how charming, how great it would be to be afloat out of your body. Keep feeling/imagining as though you are floating.

This projection technique often needs an aid to imagine this floating process. For example, you can visualize birds flying up and pulling your astral body with a string. Strongly visualize them pulling you gently out of your physical body.

This technique can be adopted with modifications; whatever suits you, the crux is you imagine that you are floating up. Gradually you will feel the vibrations but ignore them totally and continue imagining yourself floating upwards until you free yourself from the physical body.

Roll Out Technique : It is a common variation of the 'Lift' method. This is very similar, in it instead of visualizing that you are floating upward, visualize that you are rolling sideways out of your body.

Feel yourself gently rolling from side to side. Initially feel rolling slowly and then gradually build the momentum. Ultimately, you will reach that critical point where you will really roll out of your physical body.

5. *Object Technique*

This is a great technique to enhance your concentration and visualization skills and it takes around ten minutes only to perform.

This technique is a brilliant exercise to focus and maintain your awareness away from your physical body.

Choose an object in your home which should be physical and relatively easy to visualize and in a different room from the room you use for your Astral Projection techniques.

You can select any physical object like a painting, bed, chair, sofa, sculpture or anything else that has some special meaning to you. Feel and memorize the sensations that are associated with your walk up to that object and repeat your walk a number of times until you can simply remember the smallest details of that object.

The crux of this technique is to focus and preserve your attention away from your physical body when you drift off to sleep.

6. *Affirmations Technique*

The idea behind affirmations is to condition the mind by repeating something to implant a suggestion into your sub-conscious mind. If through the whole day and while going to sleep, if you repeat the following affirmations or any of your own, you can boost the chance of having a Lucid Dream or OBE.

'Tonight I will surely go

out-of-body

&

I will also remember

Everything upon

waking."

"I will have an out-of-body experience,

Even if I sleep,

I'll have my waking consciousness,

I will consciously leave my body,

With full recall of the experience."

As much your sub-conscious will get saturated with affirmations that much chances of success will be enhanced.

7. *Red Spot Technique*

This is a very simple but a great technique. This technique must be used after several hours of sleep. When you wake up, keep your body still, eyes closed and don't move your limbs. Imagine a big Red Spot near your bed on the floor and visualize yourself sitting on that big Red Spot.

The idea is to sleep again but with a particular goal in your mind. Keep this idea strongly rooted in your mind as you fall asleep again.

If you have a firm will, soon you'll be aware that your Astral Body has fallen to the floor.

The heart of this technique is that you firmly imagine that you are on the floor next to your bed.

8. *Stretch-out Technique*

Lie down on your bed with closed eyes and relaxed body. Imagine your feet are stretching out and becoming longer by an inch or more. After that, feel yourself normal. Then feel your head is stretching out and becoming longer by an inch and then again feel normal.

Now stretch your head and feet alternately. This will gradually increase the distance about two-three feet or more. Now visualize stretching out both together. This will make you very long.

Now picture yourself gradually becoming very large, bulging up, swelling and filling the whole room like a vast balloon.

With practice of this technique, you will start experiencing floating sensations and then you can order your sub-conscious mind to rise up towards the ceiling.

The timing of this technique depends upon person to person like some people just take five minutes only to complete the whole process while some take 15-20 minutes.

9. Trampoline Technique

You can use this technique with your favourite breathing exercise. You have to visualize yourself jumping up and down continually and jump a bit higher with every bounce. Gradually as your consciousness will get farther and farther away from your body, you will begin to feel separated. When you start feeling the motion, let yourself drift off into sleep, and still don't think of anything except how that motion feels. By concentrating long enough on the jumping movement, it will trigger vibrations. Trampoline is a great technique based on movement.

10. Astral Projection from Lucid Dreams

In Lucid dreams the dreamer remains aware that he is dreaming. Actually Lucid Dreams are the gateway to Astral Projection.

In this technique one needs to condition his mind to have Lucid dreams and achieve projection through Lucid dreams. This can be done by affirmations and becoming obsessed with the idea that you can achieve them. 'Strong Desire' is the key.

In every free moment you must tell your mind that you will remain conscious in your dreams.

Write the word 'LUCID' on your hand so you will remember every time you see your hand, and keep repeating your affirmation "Tonight I'll have a Lucid Dream". Ask yourself many times during the day, "Am I dreaming?"

While going to sleep look at your hands and remind yourself that you will have Lucid dreams.

All this will programme your sub-conscious to induce a Lucid Dream.

In a Lucid Dream actually a person is already 'out' of his body. Once anyone masters this method, he can simply enter the Astral realm by becoming lucid in a dream.

♦♦♦

Chapter 5

Astral Planes & Astral World

Astral Plane

Plane means a level of existence. Yet we are a multi-dimensional entity and we have a part of ourselves in different planes but our consciousness is focused on physical plane and mostly we ignore the other existences. We just think of ourselves as a man composed of blood and flesh. Every plane has some specific attributes, yet the astral plane is a doorway to access other planes or we can say that it's like an extension of the physical plane, a transitional plane.

Astral plane is reflection of all the things that occur in the physical plane. Everything existing on our physical plane or earth first originates in the Astral plane. Therefore, the Astral world is timeless, spaceless, infinite and eternal without any start or end. Everything present in the material world must exist first in the Astral world.

As humans, we are on the physical plane for Learning through feelings, thoughts and emotions.

Astral planes are actually elementary to the creation of everything that had ever existed or is existing or will ever exist in the physical world. During sleep, we explore other planes also. The fluidity of those planes allows us to create easily without the restriction of our physical plane.

Planes of Existence

Most commonly it is believed that there are seven planes of our existence. Every plane has different frequency, density and vibrations. Higher the frequency of vibrations, higher the plane.

First Plane

(Physical)

We all are familiar with this plane as this is the plane on which we currently live in. It contains physical matter like solid, liquid, gas, atoms, plants, animal's bodies and human bodies.

Second Plane

(Astral)

It is called emotional plane because on this plane all dreams, hopes, desires can be fulfilled. It is the belief that after our physical death we spend some time on Astral plane before moving to a higher plane.

On this plane the aspects of time and space are very much distorted. An hour passed in this plane can only be a few minutes on the physical plane.

On this realm several mythological creatures dwell like lower orders of devas or angels, and nature-spirits or elements (good and bad) such as fairies. On this plane we can come across inhabitants of a non-human nature also, which are just beyond the powers of human vision.

Third Plane

(Mental)

On this plane time is even more distorted than Astral plane. Here time can be just a moment long or a century long in terms of earthly time. On this plane all thoughts and ideas are manifest into actual objects.

After completing its work on Astral Plane the soul moves to the next subdivision of the higher plane, i.e., mental plane.

Fourth Plane

(Buddhic)

Once any soul reaches this plane it will most likely wish to stay here only as this plane is full of love and peace.

Fifth Plane

(Spiritual)

On this plane a person loses his individuality. Here a person gets a very high level of spiritual knowledge. This plane is very hard to reach.

Sixth Plane

(Monadic)

On this plane all the things are tied together, all paradoxes lost here.

Seventh Plane

(Adi)

This plane can't be expressed in words. It is the highest plane of everything with complete oneness.

As the level of plane becomes higher it becomes that much hardest to reach on that realm. Still these are the Seven Planes possible to reach.

I would honestly like to tell my readers that still I have not gone beyond Second Plane that is Astral. Otherwise I would have better explained other planes too.

Astral World & Astral Entities

In Astral World all kind of life forms resides, with different levels of intelligence.

We can come across all these entities and even interact with some of them. We may find some of Astral inhabitants friendly and some hostile. Be sure these Astral Entities can't harm us whatsoever they are.

In Astral Plane we can come across three types of entities:

1. Human Entities
2. Non-human Entities
3. Artificial Entities

Human Entities

We can meet people who are Unconsciously Astral Travelling. They may be Sleepers and not conscious of being in Astral Plane. They have no control on their thoughts. If we meet any known traveller in Astral plane who is wandering there unconsciously, he/she may not respond to us or on waking may just remember a dream of meeting you. While travelling on Astral plane in dreams one can meet any sort of experience, good or bad. Most of us do unconscious Astral Travel. We take our pleasant Astral experience as a sweet dream and unpleasant as nightmare.

Those people who consciously travel can get the benefit of Astral Projection. They can meet spiritual guides and they can better remember their Astral Experiences. Those who are dead can be met on Astral realm. If our dead loved ones exist on the same plane then we can even communicate with them.

Sometimes it happens that two Conscious Astral Projectors meet each other in Astral plane and consciously talk to each other and exchange each other's addresses, names and then make contact on physical plane.

Non-human Entities

Non-human entities like angels, fairies, nature spirits, and elves also dwell in Astral World. Some non-human entities may be bad and some may be good.

Bad entities like devils, ghosts, demons are found only in the lowest regions of the Lower Astral. If we encounter any bad entity during that time, we must know that they can't harm us. They frighten weak people. If we will command them to move away, then they will go. We can even come across Astral body of animals also.

Artificial Entities

Artificial entities are not real or natural. Rather they are created by our thoughts. They are manifestation of our own desires, thoughts and fears. Sometimes they may scare us but always remember that they can't harm us.

That's why it is required for projectors to control their thoughts as much as possible. New astral projectors fear more. So they are more likely to encounter such artificial entities more than experienced ones.

♦♦♦

Chapter 6

Pre-Projection Phenomena

A number of sensations and events are general to people who try Astral Projection or Out-of-body experiences. Even though there is likeness between people's experiences, they are by no means exactly the same. It is rare to find any individual who experiences all of such sensations; equally so, it's rare to find someone who doesn't experience any of the sensations at all.

Individual variations and difference in intensity of some sensations also occur, from person to person. Even in a single individual, each projection attempt might produce different sensations, with different intensity and in a different sequence.

Whatever differences or intensity these pre-projection sensations have, they continue to give us confirmation that we are on the right track.

Some Common Pre-Projection Sensations

1. *Vibrations*

Whilst attempting Astral Projection 'Vibrations' can occur spontaneously. Vibrations are a very common phenomenon, but a few people claim that they have never experienced the vibrations.

Along with vibrations some other feelings like numbness, intense shaking, paralysis, noises like buzzing, humming or gunshot sound may be felt.

Many people get so panicked by such sensations that they come out of their trance state. Actually vibrations are caused because of the flow of energy through Chakras, and due to attempt of Astral body to come out of the physical body.

Vibrations show that you are on the right track. So when you feel vibrations while projecting then just remain totally calm and relaxed. Vibrations don't harm you at all. Rather it can be used as a tool to achieve projection.

2. *Sleep Paralysis*

Sleep Paralysis is the state when in your sleep you suddenly find yourself unable to move or speak and feel your body 'paralyzed' to the extent that even you cannot move any part of your body at all. You might feel some weight on your chest.

Your physical body will seemingly become completely 'paralyzed' to the extent that you simply cannot seem to budge/move any part of your body at all.

Do not be anxious if this happens as you are absolutely safe. Rather it is a state when Astral body is very close to the actual exit. Once you are in sleep paralysis, you can be out of the body in seconds with very little effort. In such state just relax and take deep breaths and with each deep breath, imagine yourself rising up, now you have great chances to get out of your physical body.

However, if you are just partially paralyzed, silence your mind and relax. As you relax, your paralysis will become stronger and then you can will yourself out of the physical body.

3. *Buzzing and Other Sounds*

Before leaving the body, you may encounter a mixture of noises, whose nature may be related to your own characteristics, personality, experiences and perception.

Initially such sounds may frighten you but with experience you get used to them. These sounds are like – buzzing, whooshing, loud bell, rushing, gunshot, roaring, explosions or bird screeching, a chime being struck, knocking, thumping, clapping and voices of people talking.

Among these sounds buzzing is a very common pre-projection symptom and it can intensify so much that one can feel a hundred helicopters in his ears! But these are temporary symptoms and they collapse when the separation process is complete.

One should not get terrified by such sounds but rather understand that they prove to you that you are right on track.

4. *Hallucinations*

Some hallucinations can also occur while projecting or even in normal sleep. Generally they occur with sleep paralysis. Hallucinations which occur before sleep are called hypnagogic, and hallucinations which occur after waking up are termed as hypnopompic. There can be both kind of audio or visual hallucinations, for example, songs, music, footsteps, some specific sounds of technological devices, such as TV, radio, typewriter, or natural sounds like water flowing, wind blowing, leaves rustling, animal noises. Visual hallucinations like seeing colours, lights, faces of known and unknown people, scenes of anything imaginable, etc.

These hallucinations mostly occur because of the overlap of dreaming and wakefulness. So there is no need to be scared of them.

5. *Sensing a Presence*

At some point in our life, generally all of us feel a presence of someone else, whereas actually there is no one else around. It is not a unique phenomenon to pre-projection, rather a common phenomenon. Though, sensing a presence usually happens during sleep paralysis, so these two phenomena are in some way linked.

The reason for sensing this presence is basically a matter of belief. The biological interpretation says that the brain starts to dream, and creates feelings and thoughts that are beyond the physical reality.

Some occult theories suggest the existence of spiritual guides or ancestors in the case of kind entities; unknown spirits in the case of neutral entities; and attributions of evil spirits in cases of vicious presences.

6. *Weight Changes*

One may feel change in his weight which occurs, often quite suddenly.

Weight Changes generally occur in two stages. One stage is when body enters in deep relaxation, and the other is when sleep paralysis occurs. In both cases, one can feel extremely weighty or extremely light weight. Generally deep body relaxation is linked with heaviness, and sleep paralysis gives lightness.

7. *Temperature Changes*

Generally during sleep our body temperature drops a fraction. During projection since the consciousness becomes detached from body, it also causes change in body temperature.

8. *Movement Sensations*

When the Astral body starts to separate from the physical body, the movement sensations like feelings of falling or flying, slight dizziness, vertigo, feelings of rocking or swaying can also occur.

9. *Rapid Heart Rate*

Rapid Heart rate is a very common Pre-projection symptom. There may be many reasons to it, like opening of heart chakra, may be due to fear or excitement or it may be due to the knowledge of the heart-beat shifting.

Whatever reason it is, the projector should remain passive and calm.

10. *Breathing Changes*

Breathing Changes is also a common symptom of the soul/body separation. Sometimes one may feel shortness of breath, or feelings of not breathing, but he should not panic. Actually breathing isn't stopping, but the consciousness of it is.

11. Eye Movements

During lucid dreaming or separation state, generally eye moves to the left and right, indicating that the brain has started creating dreams. It is also called Rapid Eye Movement.

12. Blackout

Sometimes when exit sensations like vibrations, breathlessness, and rapid heart beating reach a seemingly intolerable degree, some people suddenly find themselves losing consciousness for some seconds. They reach to a state of "void", from where any scene can be created.

13. Waking Paralysis

Waking Paralysis state happens when partial projection occurs. Yet some degree of physical paralysis is a sure sign of a projection in progress due to mind split effect. The degree of paralysis depends mostly upon the strength of the projection and the flow of energy used to maintain it.

In such situation the projector should relax and use a projection technique so that a full projection can then occur.

Many people find it a very terrifying experience but it is not dangerous at all. By concentrating on any limb like a single big toe and trying hard to move it the waking paralysis can be broken.

14. Heavy Exit Sensations

Heavy exit sensations like vibration, rapid heartbeat etc. quickly decreases after the first few conscious projections.

The energy body gradually becomes used to the conscious projection process, and progressively adapts and develops further for conscious Astral Projections.

15. Lost Focus During the Exit

During exit process due to heavy sensations the projector may fail to shift the 'centre' of consciousness out of the physical body. During exit it is very essential for a projector to keep his mind clear and focused.

If attention slips during exit then astral body may project out without a strong centre of waking consciousness. Due to this, the projector's strongest centre of consciousness will remain locked inside the physical body.

This may create double memories because of the mind split effect causing problems for projectors or in the majority of cases, no memory of the successful projection remains upon waking up.

♦♦♦

Chapter 7

Post-Projection Basics

In Astral World the World is yours. You are the creator, so control and watch your thoughts very carefully.

1. Silver Cord

The Silver cord is a silver colour flowing, elastic but a strong connecting cord which connects Astral body to its Physical body.

The Silver cord can never be detached during Astral Projection. It only severs when death occurs.

The Silver cord gets connected to our physical body for the first time when we are born, and it only severs at the final moment, i.e., at the time of death.

The Silver cord remains thick and short when Astral and Physical bodies are very close to each other. As the distance increases, the cord becomes thinner and longer. The Silver cord has the ability to be stretched till infinity, which means that we can go up to any distance, anywhere in the universe and yet it will not break.

2. Control Your Thoughts

It is very essential to hold full control over your thoughts and emotions at all times during Astral projection because you yourself are the creator of your Astral world. Any thought during Astral Projection is instantly manifested because Astral world is greatly responsive to feelings, like if we fear then we have a possibility of meeting an evil being. Yet being a product of your own imagination it can't harm you in real. So there is no need to fear.

3. Communication During Astral Projection

Communication on the Astral Plane is done telepathically. There is no language barrier. Due to telepathy every soul can understand every other soul. Such non-verbal communication can take place between you and any other kind of living entity, whether that is human or non-human. Such telepathic communications are very effective because in it a lot of information can be exchanged in a fraction of a second. Because it's a non-verbal communication, the chances of misinterpretation are highly diminished and the messages received are very accurate and such communication may be very mind-expanding too.

4. Movement on the Astral Plane

There is no gravity in Astral Realm and no restriction on movements like those in our physical body. Yet, due to our life-long conditioning, we might try to move by walking as we normally do in the Physical body.

In the Astral world, this is an inept way of motion, because in Astral realm we can easily fly or glide at our will.

Even in Astral world we can reach at any place or to any person just by 'thinking' but it requires practice and great control over thoughts. Sometimes mysterious 'Astral Currents' can take you somewhere without your will. But with a strong will, you can reach where you wish to.

5. Astral Vision

With our human body we can see only in front of us and sideways partially as our physical body has around 220 degrees of vision.

During Astral projection all our senses get enhanced, including our vision. Our Astral body has a spherical vision of 360-degrees which means that during Astral Projection we can see in any direction even behind our back.

But here the biggest hurdle is that as our brain is lifelong conditioned for having frontal vision only. So for us it becomes very hard to adjust to or come to terms with spherical vision.

So to use the 360-degree vision we need a lot of practice.

6. Astral Blindness

Astral Blindness or blurred Astral vision is a common phenomenon of Astral Projection. This happens especially with new inexperienced projectors. But there is nothing to be worried about it.

Generally this happens when the projector remains too close to his body (around within 15 feet).

As his astral body shifts away, his vision improves. So, to avoid this Astral blindness, the best thing the projector can do is to move further away from his physical body.

Mentally the projector should ask the eyes like voluntarily commanding himself 'Vision Now'.

7. Duality

In Duality effect a person remains aware of his Physical body simultaneously with the awareness of his Astral body at a different location.

Duality occurs because of mind split.

This concept has been confirmed by a number of Astral Projectors; even I myself have experienced it.

8. Nourishment and Clothing during Astral Projection

It is not required to nourish the Astral form or eat, drink, etc. The astral body itself soaks the life-giving fluid energy flowing through the astral ethers.

Some people often wonder how we remain during astral projection... naked or are we clothed? It actually depends upon our own perception, if we perceive ourselves naked then we see ourselves naked and if we visualize us in clothes then we find us wearing clothes.

Usually we find ourselves wearing the same clothes which our physical body is wearing at that time and moreover most of the times while projecting we don't much care what clothes we are wearing.

9. Returning Back to Physical Body

This is the last and easiest step of Astral projection because even if you don't want to return you will come back to your body!

One can have Abrupt Return to his body or a Controlled return.

When you want to return to your physical body no matter where you are in the Astral realm, just think about your Physical body and next moment you will find yourself already there. This is a controlled return. After entering your body just keep your eyes closed for a few moments and try to recall all your recent Astral experiences.

♦♦♦

Chapter 8

Related Concepts

1. Third Eye

The Third Eye is also known as the Inner Eye. Third eye is a very important concept particularly in Hinduism related to the Ajna (brow) chakra. The third eye is frequently associated with clairvoyance, ability to observe chakras and auras, and Astral experiences.

When the Etheric Body gets sufficient Cosmic Energy by more and more Meditation our Third Eye gets activated and we start perceiving crystal clear visions of this plane and other planes. During the activation of the Third Eye, we feel an itching sensation or pulling sensation at the forehead region. When we are in 'No Thought' state and connected to the Source, our Third Eye gets activated.

When our Third Eye activates we hear clear, vibrating sounds, see visions of Masters, Lights, Auras and much more. We also feel the knowledge behind the Experiences. Third Eye Experience helps to solve one's problems as this experience gives us immense knowledge.

2. Etheric Matter

It is a matter in between Physical matter and Astral matter. Etheric Matter is the actual Life Force Substance generated by all living things. It is part physical and part astral. Etheric matter is scientifically proved and has actual weight. In all the cases of the exact moment of death, a sudden weight loss of approximately one quarter of an ounce is recorded. This happens because at the time of physical death a large amount of etheric matter is transferred into the astral body.

3. Doppelganger Phenomena

Doppelganger phenomena means doubling of a living person. It is a very rare phenomenon. Only a very small percentage of Astral Projectors claim to have experienced the doppelganger phenomena. This effect is most likely to occur while sleeping or Astral Projecting rather than when being completely awake. According to Doppelganger phenomena a person appears to people in a place where he is not present. This appearance usually occurs in a place they frequent and would normally be at, such as at their home or at work. Such doppelganger can be engaged in conversation, and they have full knowledge and memories of it. Whereas the actual person who is in a completely different place has no knowledge, memory of that event. He can later discover it when someone tells him. I personally believe that it is a very rare occurrence.

4. Remote Viewing

Remote viewing (RV) means viewing distant or unseen thing using paranormal means. By our extra-sensory perception (ESP) we can see a place or event happening presently but happening distantly. Astral Projection can be used as a tool for remote viewing. Remote viewers can see objects and scenes hundreds or thousands of miles away by closing their eyes and focusing on the object or place.

5. Near Death Experience (NDE)

So many cases have been recorded about Near Death Experiences. Near death experience happens when a person is almost near to dying or sometimes declared clinically dead whereas during that period he actually is undergoing an 'out-of-body' experience. Some people who experience an NDE report being able to do Astral Projection afterwards, or find that Astral Projection becomes possible for them.

6. Spontaneous Projection

Spontaneous projection generally occurs while trying to sleep, while sleeping, during meditation, or as part of an NDE. It is just Astral Projecting without any effort or even wanting to Astral Project. The more we project, the more likely the occurrence of spontaneous projections. A few people naturally experience spontaneous projections during their entire life.

7. Lucid Dreaming

A lucid dream means dreaming while knowing that we are dreaming. If during any dream a person is aware that he is dreaming then such kind of dream is a Lucid Dream. A lot of the information that deals with Astral Projection deals with lucid dreaming too. Also Astral Projection from a lucid dream is very easy to do.

8. Dreamwalking

Dreamwalking means moving into another's dream. There are various ways of dreamwalking from both, an Astral Projection and from a Lucid Dreaming state.

9. Akashic Records

Akashic Records are records of every thought and event that has ever occurred. It is a zone between Astral and Mental worlds. The Akashic Records are like imprint of all experiences of all lifetime in all realities. Akashic Records are an etheric, holographic repository of information for human consciousness for the past, present and potentials for the future.

They are a collection of everything that has occurred in the past, and they also have a complete set of information regarding future. Every individual has its own, unique Akashic Record. Our personal Akashic Records contain every piece of information regarding us about our past lives, relationships, health, our soul path, and all other details.

Some people while projecting have claimed to have entered the Akashic Records and found something like a library there, with real books with records of their past, present and future as a text book.

10. Death

Death happens when the Silver Cord breaks and the spirit leaves the body forever. In first few days, the soul of dead one projects close to the physical world, then it enters in the Astral plane. There the spirit fulfils all the desires that he have ever wanted to fulfil as a human.

After saturating with every need and desire, and finding that those desires were actually the illusions, the spirit sheds the Astral (desire body) and enters in the Mental dimension, where the past life, past actions, past thoughts can be examined and expressed. The Akashic Record exists on this dimension.

After shedding mental body the soul enters the Buddhic dimension for rest, healing, atonement, and understanding of self. On Buddhic dimension the spirit becomes perfect.

Then the soul enters the Atmic dimension and there it waits in the divine presence of loved ones. Then, finally it goes to the next level of existence, where the last and the amazing mystery of life is revealed.

11. REM (Rapid Eye Movement)

Rapid Eye Movement is generally called the 'REM' state. This state comes when physical body falls into a much deeper sleep but the mind remains conscious. The REM state signifies the ideal time to have a lucid dream, because in this state the dream mind becomes very active.

Those who are unable to project due to fear or some reason should try to have lucid dreams and then project through lucid dreams. This is because a lucid dream can be converted into a Real Time or an Out-of-body experience.

12. Spirits

Personally, I do not advise astral projectors to call 'unknown spirits and guides' to help them. Calling blindly for such help may confront you with a risk. By calling

Unknown spirits you unknowingly give them permission to interfere into your life.

However you can call them about whom you know exactly or you can ask for protection from the deity you worship.

13. Calling For Help

It is possible to take help of any experienced projector when you are attempting to project. Once you reach the trance state, then mentally call out the person's name (whose help you wish to seek) many times, as loudly (mentally) as you can. If at that time he is out of his body then he will definitely hear you, no matter how far away he is and he will be drawn to visit you. However he may not be able to actually 'pull' you out of your body but if you are already out or about to project then he can help in other ways, like making you aware that you are projecting, or helping you to remember it.

Another projector can't practically pull you from your physical body as because any attempt to do so will be like a psychic attack (may produce unpleasant cold shivers, etc.) and this will tend to break his balanced 'projectable' state also. He can best help you by waiting for your natural projection to happen and then guide you.

Some experienced projectors also project jointly.

14. Developing Clairvoyance

Through practice the natural ability of clairvoyance can be improved. Clairvoyance requires a lot of visualization. There are various techniques to improve visualization.

Here I am explaining a simple technique. First close your eyes and picturize your surroundings in your mind. Then open your eyes and compare it with your mental imaginary. When you see from your physical eyes make sure to gaze at everything like a child sees everything for the first time. Let the vividness of colour and form burn into you, until everything takes on a veritable glow. Try to capture that glow when you close your eyes and now picture your surroundings. Let the brightness of colours and forms glow into you, until everything takes on a real glow. Now again close your eyes and try to capture that glow and again picture your surroundings. Now extend your mental vision to the next room, then the next building, the next city, or even the whole world. Don't expcct exact results, especially initially. Try to be at least partly right.

15. The Aura

The human aura is the energy field that surrounds the body as a coloured glow of light. A psychic who can see the aura can determine that person's emotional state. Different groups may attribute different meanings to the colours. The colours I am illustrating here are emotional in nature:

Colors of the Aura and their Nature

Black	–	malice
Dark Gray	–	depression
Pale Gray	–	fear
Brown	–	materialism

Muddy Gray	-	selfishness
Red	-	energy
Bright Red	-	anger and force
Dirty Red	-	passion and sensuality
Dull Red	-	selfish love
Rose	-	unselfish love
Orange	-	pride
Orange Cloud	-	irritability
Bright Orange	-	noble indignation
Yellow	-	intellect
Yellow-green	-	low intellect
Earthy Yellow	-	selfish thought
Lemon	-	high intellect
Bright Gold	-	logical thinking
Bright Red-yellow	-	spiritual thought
Green	-	empathy
Gray-green	-	deceit, jealously
Greenish-brown	-	jealousy
Emerald Green	-	unselfish resourcefulness
Foliage Green	-	sympathy & empathy
Bright Apple-green	-	strong vitality
Bright Turquoise	-	deep sympathy & compassion
Blue	-	devotion (religious feeling)
Gray-blue	-	fetishism
Light Blue	-	noble spiritual devotion

Dark blue	-	religious feeling
Bright Lilac-blu	-	lofty religious idealism
Violet	-	spiritual psychic & spiritual faculty
White	-	purity/protection

16. Affirmations

An affirmation works exactly like a hypnotist's patter. Affirmations are positive suggestions, more like commands, which we affirm or repeat to ourselves (for example, *"I can do Astral Projection."*).

Our sub-conscious mind is always open to suggestions. Our conscious mind works as a censor but Affirmations are the way to break through the censor.

If we wish to change or develop any quality within our self, then an affirmation is ideal. Give your mind the same suggestion several times a day, especially when you go to bed. Affirmations are subtle and it may require a few months to impact.

♦♦♦

Chapter 9

Lucid Dreaming

What is Lucid Dreaming?

A Lucid Dream means dreaming while knowing that we are dreaming. If during any dream a person is aware that he is dreaming then such kind of dream is a Lucid Dream. In a lucid dream, the dreamer may be able to exert some degree of control over their participation within the dream or be able to manipulate their imaginary experiences in the dream environment. This term was coined by Frederik van Eeden, a Dutch psychiatrist and writer. Lucid dreaming is researched scientifically, and it's a well established phenomenon.

The super hit movie, ***Inception***, which is written and directed by a real life lucid dreamer, Chris Nolan, has popularized the concept of lucid dreaming and became an inspiration for so many Lucid Dreamers.

Some people are good at recalling their regular dreams. The dream recall provides them memories of secret inner worlds and creates understanding about the sub-conscious mind. Lucid dreams may be vivid and realistic. Though, the quality of lucidity of dreams may vary greatly. When dreams are highly lucid, we remain aware that everything which is happening in the dream is actually occurring in our mind and there is no real danger. In low-level lucid dreams we can be aware to a certain extent only that we are dreaming. Whereas high-level lucid dreams take one huge leap further – to a fantasy land where everything we see, taste, hear, smell or feel can be as real as our waking reality. With conscious dream control, we can explore our private dreamscape like a virtual reality world.

The Benefits of Lucid Dreaming

Listening to the concept of Lucid Dreams, people often ask, *"Why do we have lucid dreams? What are their benefits?"*

Here I have compiled a list of potential benefits of Lucid Dreaming:

1. Overcoming Nightmares

Dreams provide an outlet for unlimited fantasy and pleasure, but unluckily for many people dreams are frightening episodes of never-ending terror. Nightmares reduces the quality of life, causes less sleep, painful memories, induces fear and thus decreases self-confidence.

The greatest benefits of Lucid Dreams are observed on such people who suffer frequent nightmares. When we know that we are dreaming, it is a simple logical step of realizing that nothing is real and we are absolutely safe. In lucid dreams when we face the fear and frightening things knowing that they can't harm us, it increases our self-confidence and makes us stronger in our real life too.

2. *Wish Fulfilment*

Russou had quoted that 'Man is born free but everywhere he is in ties'. In our real life we have so many social, physical, cultural limitations and boundaries that sometimes we feel so very suffocated.

Lucid dreams can give us an outlet and opportunity to crack the bonds of reality. In Lucid dreams we can live by our rules. We are only restricted by our power of imagining.

We can effectively utilise the time recovered from sleeping. Most of the people sleep an average of eight hours per day. Lucid dreaming can help us use that time according to our wish and actually experience life the way we have always dreamed of.

3. *Emotional Benefits*

Many lucid dreamers use lucid dreaming techniques to motivate and inspire themselves through their dreams. Like a nightmare can induce stress and give our day a bad start, a motivating and pleasing dream can keep us happy and motivated throughout the day.

4. *Adventure and Fantasy*

With the tool of Lucid Dreaming we can fulfil all our wild fantasies. Many lucid dreamers say that their first lucid dream was the most amazing experience of their lives. In our dreamscape we can do any adventure we wish to do, without getting harmed. We can fly, have sex, do all the pleasurable things and best thing is that there will be no social or physical consequences of our actions.

5. *Ahead of Entertainment*

Lucid dreaming is not just only a source of endless entertainment. Rather it is an amazing tool which can be used for many things like - recalling old memories, preparing our self for important tasks in advance, reinforcing our education or learning about anything.

6. *Rehearsal*

In lucid dreaming, by forming of mental imagery we can rehearse things for real life as the activity of the brain during a dream activity remains same during the real event also. Example: Any artistic performance, public speaking, any difficult confrontation or athletic competence.

7. *Transcendence*

Exalted and ecstatic states are common to occur in lucid dreams. Lucid dreaming may be proved as a gateway to great peace, spiritual teaching, achieving states of union with the Almighty, and understanding the purpose of life. Thus Lucid Dreaming is a source of transcendent experience.

8. *Healing*

Imaginary healing in dreams may improve physical and mental health. Visual imagery healing on the body and its positive effects are a well-established concept. So many lucid dreamers use lucid dreams in overcoming phobias, decreasing social and sexual anxieties, problem solving, relaxing mind, overcoming pain and fear, achieving greater self-confidence and directing the mind and body in the dream to facilitate physical healing.

9. Problem Solving and Creativity

During REM sleep our brain becomes highly active and creative. There are so many memories and things in our sub-conscious mind. Dreams are the key to open the storehouse of our brain. Using the facts and information we had forgotten and with expanded mental capabilities by using Lucid Dreaming we can solve our problems in better ways.

Lucid dreams can be great help to artists. Entering into the fantasy realm during Lucid Dreams the artists, painters, writers can come up with their masterpiece.

We can consciously ask questions to our self in our lucid dreams and seek their answers and then command our subconscious mind and body to act accordingly. For example:

- What should I do to solve my problems?
- What wrongs have I committed in my life?
- What is the ultimate aim of my life?
- What should I do to become rich?
- What should be my ideal career?

Prerequisites for Lucid Dreaming

Everyone who is normal is capable of lucid dreaming but there are certain prerequisites for achieving Lucid Dreams:

√ Sufficient amount of sleep is absolutely vital.

√ For achieving Lucid Dream we must experience REM sleep (sleep in which dreaming occurs). Eight hours of sleeping will be sufficient for REM sleep.

- √ Like learning any skill, lucid dreaming skill also requires time and effort. Regular Practice, Diligence, determination is the key.

Steps of Lucid Dreaming

The Four Basic Steps are as follows:

1. **Mental Preparation**
2. **Dream Recall**
3. **Dream Understanding**
4. **Dream Awareness**

1. Mental Preparation

Positive attitude and affirmations are very crucial for Lucid Dreaming. For building a mental framework to maximize the success includes positive affirmations like:

- √ I strongly believe that I can develop the ability to lucid dream.
- √ I believe lucid dreams are important.
- √ I really want to have lucid dreams.
- √ I know what I will do when I will become lucid.

Such affirmations play a crucial role to mould our belief system and to manage our thoughts. Make your dreams your priority and try to recall them, try to understand them. Cultivate a strong desire for lucid dreaming. Be positive and replace doubt with belief. This kind of mental conditioning will surely help to speed up the lucid dreaming process.

2. Dream Recall

Forgetting our dreams makes it hard to have lucid dreams. Some people have good ability to recall their dreams whereas some don't. But that's not a big deal. There are so many tried and tested ways to remember the dreams.

But the prerequisite is a right mindset. One should have a strong desire to have lucid dreams, belief in lucid dreaming and making it a conscious priority.

Below I am mentioning some effective tips for increasing dream recall that will help in remembering more and more of dreams only with a few weeks' practice. The following techniques are just required to be incorporated into our morning schedule.

1. Wake Up Slowly & Motionlessly

When you wake up then don't move or open your eyes. Just lie completely motionless and concentrate your mind on remembering your dreams. You may have seen so many dreams while asleep that this may flood your mind. Just try to concentrate on whatever you were dreaming as you woke up. We can best recall our dream while lying in the same position in which wc were while dreaming.

2. Chose your best Sleeping Position

Test and try all your sleeping positions and then choose the position which is best suited to you for your dream recall.

3. Keep Trying

It might be possible that we may not recall our dream when we wake up but flashes of the dream may surface later. We must write down such dream memories.

4. Allow your Mind to Remember

Allow your mind to drift and leave it free to ponder and receive whatever mental imagery it can form. Recall of any one part of dream becomes helpful in remembering the whole dream.

5. Dream Checklist

Sometimes we don't get any hue of what we were dreaming. In such case we can make a dream checklist in our mind. Dream Checklist may include people, places, activities, smell, music, incidents, anything. You can concentrate and think whether a particular person, thing or a place was there in your dream or not. Think about the kind of movement (dancing, walking, running, sitting, climbing or flying) or emotions (laughing, happy, sad, afraid, surprised) you were experiencing in your dreams. Try to question yourself backward as one dream fragment usually leads to another.

6. Alarm Clock Method

Those who face much difficulty in dream recall they must try this method. While sleeping we can set the alarm for the time when we are most likely to dream. We may find fresh memories of our dream in our mind during those moments.

We can use Alarm Clock method in different ways like:

- Set the alarm for two hours earlier than you usually wake up. This is called Early Morning Method.
- Odd Hour Alarm Method – Throughout the night alarm can be set at any random times. This method makes you an eager learner for developing your lucid dreaming skills.
- We can also use 'Snooze Alarm Button'. It makes constantly coming in and coming out of dreams possible thereby dramatically increasing dream recall.

6. Keeping a Dream Journal

It is the most important thing to develop dream recall and progress in lucid dreaming. The habit of writing down your dreams readily helps recalling your dreams.

The following tips can be kept in mind while maintaining a Dream Journal:

- √ Date & time must be included in each dream journal entry.
- √ You should include, if you can, a title for each dream.
- √ A suitable title or name can be given to the dream according to what we saw in our dream.
- √ It is advised to write dream entries in present tense instead of using past tense as it helps in remembering the dream better while writing.
- √ Before writing we must try to recall the dream fully in our mind. Then while writing probably we will recall more.
- √ Space can be left in each dream entry so that late arriving memories can be written down.
- √ Sketches of dreams can be drawn on one side of your diary.

3. Dreams Understanding

When we succeed in recalling our dreams then naturally we start becoming more familiar with our Dreams. We start noticing that certain people, places and things appear more in our dreams. We will observe repetition of same pattern and theme of our dreams. Slowly we start noticing our Dream Signs. We must write down these Dream Signs. These dream signs help us in dream recall and lucid dreaming and enhance our analysis about ourselves and our dreams.

4. *Dream Awareness*

This is the final step to become aware of dreaming, i.e., while dreaming we know that we are dreaming and we can manipulate our dream according to our wish. There are many ways to increase our awareness like:

√ While dreaming ask yourself 'Am I dreaming?'

√ Try to remain aware of your consciousness as if you are just an observer. The longer the awareness can be sustained, the better will be the lucid dream.

√ Meditation is an excellent way to sustain our awareness. Studies show that people who meditate have a greater possibility of having lucid dreams.

√ To learn lucid dreaming we must be able to differentiate between 'reality' and 'dream'. We can do reality checks by following undermentioned tips:

- Ask yourself whether you are dreaming or not.
- Look at the clock and observe whether it stays constant or not.
- Pinch your nose closed and try to breathe.
- Jump in the air, usually we start flying during dreams.
- Look into a mirror. In dreams usually our images don't reflect or appear blurred or distorted.
- Switch on-off any electric button.

Lucid Dreaming Tips

1. After you wake up remember to ask yourself several times a day "Am I dreaming?" Also perform reality checks.

2. Keep a Dream Journal. Put it close to your bed while sleeping and write in it immediately after waking up.

3. Know your best time of having a lucid dream. Don't disturb your sleep cycle.

4. Try to meditate more and more.

5. Go through your previous dreams in your Dream Journal. Slowly you will start noticing your dream-patterns and dream-signs.

Lucid Dreaming FAQs

Q.1. What is the relation between Lucid dreaming and Astral Projection?

Practitioners of Lucid Dreams and Astral Projection believe that there is a close relation between Lucid Dreaming and Astral Projection. Both are closely related and act as a gateway for each other because both occur at the same psychological state. Many Astral practitioners use Lucid dreaming technique for projecting and many times Lucid dreams are induced while having an OBE.

Q.2. Can any Harm or Danger be caused by Lucid Dreaming?

Researches and data show that lucid dreams almost in all the cases have positive and pleasing experiences. With positive attitude in Lucid Dreaming we can see positive results as our behaviour and attitude strongly influence our experience in both worlds.

Some people complain about lucidity in unpleasant dreams or nightmares. But they should try to use Lucid dreams as a tool to fight bad dreams and an overwhelming majority show that Lucid dreams have proved beneficial in overcoming nightmares.

Some people complain that the experiences of lucid dreams are so much exciting and delightful that they will become addicted and will want to sleep longer hours. But biologically that's not possible as we have a limited amount of REM sleep.

Q.3. How do we feel in Lucid Dreaming?

Some Lucid Dreamers say that their first Lucid Dream was the most amazing experience of their life. The potential of lucid dreaming is limitless. Lucid dreaming is much more than entertainment and a fantasy realm. Through Lucid dreams we can chance to interact with our own sub-conscious mind, can recall our past and can get better understanding of our life and analyze our situation in a better way.

Q.4. Is there any similarity between Lucid Dreaming and Dream Control?

Lucid Dreaming and Dream Control are not synonymous. We can be lucid in our dreams but may not be able to control them and vice versa.

Q.5. Can Lucid Dreaming be Learnt by Everyone?

Yes, it can be learnt by every normal human being. Sometimes without any intention we have spontaneous lucid dreams but they occur rarely. With specific Lucid Dreaming techniques, we can increase the quantity and quality of our dream recall and become more Lucid in dreaming.

Q.6. What are Dream Signs?

Dream Signs mean some elements in dreams that indicate that we are dreaming. By studying our dream patterns we can become familiar with our own personal dream signs and set our mind to identify them. These dream signs help in becoming lucid in future dreams.

Q.7. How can I learn Lucid Dreaming?

Intention and practice are prerequisites of learning Lucid Dreaming. Readers can try any of the methods I have mentioned and feel free to use personal variants and experiments.

Q.8. How to Remember my Dreams?

Dream recall is one of the most important prerequisite for learning lucid dreaming. This helps us to recognize our dream's features and patterns. Maintaining a dream journal and writing what we can recall immediately upon waking from the dream helps in learning Lucid Dreaming.

Q.9. Does Lucid Dreaming have Scientific Proof?

Yes. Sufficient scientific research has been done on it. There is no doubt in the validity of lucid dreaming and it is not a Paranormal Phenomenon of any kind.

Mainly there are two famous experiments which authenticate the existence of lucid dreams:

(A) Brain Frequency Recordings

During Lucid dreams brain activity increases. The results of Neurological Laboratory analysis show that lucidity is a different state of consciousness.

The EEG machine in Neurological laboratory recorded highly active frequencies (i.e Gamma range) up to the 40 Hz in lucid dreamers. Which is far more dynamic than the normal dream state (Theta: 4-8 Hz) and even greater than our waking state which is (Beta: 12-38 Hz), validating Lucid Dreams. The neurological research also showed heightened activity in the frontal areas of the brain

(B) Communication through Eye Movements in a Lucid Dream

The research of British parapsychologist, Keith Hearne also proves its validity. He experimented on a Lucid dreamer, Alan Worsley, who in a lucid dream had consciously chosen to move his eyes a certain way. This proved that Worsley was aware he was dreaming and it was a kind of communication between him and the outside world.

10. How to do Reality Testing while Lucid Dreaming?

Reality Testing is a very good technique for learning Lucid dreaming. Reality checking can be done several times a day by assigning the following exercises to yourself:

- √ Do the reality check anytime when you think of it, or when you think about dreams and do it especially when anything odd occurs.
- √ The more thorough and regular practice of this technique, the better the results.
- √ Select some particular occasions like: when you look at your watch, when you see yourself in the mirror, you reach at your home or office, or meet your best pal.
- √ Here is a good reality test: Write some text on a piece of paper and carry it with you throughout the day. To do a reality test, read the text and then look away and look back. Observing the text if you watch it changing then it's a dream state. If the characters are normal and stable then probably you are not dreaming.

♦ ♦ ♦

Chapter 10

Common Mistakes and Problems & Astral Projection Tips

You are trying hard to Project or get at least one OBE but not getting success or you are about to leave your body, feeling heavy exit vibrations and sensations but not able to exit or exit partially or have a very weak projection. Even after trying so hard you may wake up frustrated without getting results. In this chapter I will discuss such issues.

Reasons behind having Weak Astral Travel Experiences or having no Astral experience at all:

1. Attempting at Night-time

Astral Projection requires a fresh mind and body. But most aspirants try to project at night time while going to sleep. With a hectic long day their body is worn out, so they end up falling asleep or not able to focus.

Earlier I also used to commit same mistake but now I project in early morning when my body and mind are fully relaxed and fresh.

2. Fear

Only the thought of separating from the physical body frightens most aspirants. Fear is one of the biggest hurdles in OBE. Without addressing our fear we can't expect to get success in Astral Projection.

Generally the beginners have following fears regarding Astral Projection:

- **Fear of being Possessed**
- We are always safe during Projection. We have projected unconsciously so many times during sleep.
- It is never possible to get possessed during Projection. Because our Astral body and the Physical body are connected by a Silver Cord, it is not possible for any entity to break silver cord and get inside the body.
- **Fear of Death**
- Projection has nothing to do with death. Death happens only when the Silver Cord breaks but nothing can break the Silver Cord (Cord which connects Astral body to physical body) during projection.
- **Silver Cord (Thread which connects Astral body to physical body) may Break**
- Silver Cord only breaks when a person dies.
- **May Become Insane**
- This is also not possible. However, it is advised that persons suffering from mental ailment should not attempt Astral Projection.
- **Fear of Other World**
- We may fear that we may meet something nasty or some evil spirit in Astral World. Actually we are the

creators of our astral world. The Astral world is a manifestation of our own thoughts. We can create whatever we like. It's up to us whether we create good or bad. Use positive affirmations that 'I am the creator!'

- ♦ **Fear of the Unknown**
- Since Astral World is full of surprises so even after many Projections, we may have certain degree of fear of the unknown. The truth is that even while exploring unknown territories, nothing can harm us; we are invulnerable in our Astral form. Our expanded etheric will react instantly at the slightest invasion or unfriendly contact. It can pull us back in physical body in a second, no matter how far away we are.
- ♦ **Fear of Not Able to Return**
- We are unconsciously Projecting since our birth. We are yet always protected. So this is a false fear which is required to be erased from our mind. No matter how far we go, we will always come back.
- ♦ **Fear of Harm**
- We are invulnerable in our astral form and our body has excellent defence mechanism to protect us during a projection. Whenever we encounter something with malicious intent or unsafe, we can think about our physical body and immediately we will be inside.

Overcoming Fear

Those who are beginners and who do not fully understand the nature of Astral Projection they fear most. Their fears can only be over-ruled by information, knowledge and experiences. Beginners should read everything regarding Astral Projection, and become well-versed and familiar with all aspects of Astral Projection.

A few tips to overcome fear:

√ Projecting during daytime.

√ Projecting in light.

√ Joint projecting, i.e., Projecting with a friend

√ Praying to deity in which we believe for safe-guarding

√ Affirmations: Repeat these in mind:

I am totally safe. Nothing can harm me.

3. Eagerness & Impatience

Astral Projection is a lifetime experience; so it's worth waiting and trying. Astral Projection takes dedication, devotion, and a lot of patient pursuance. We must be prepared for the long time period, yet it may happen even at the first time. Conscious OBE may take months or even years to achieve. Those who expect success in days or weeks, are more than likely to give up or doubt its reality.

4. Inner Thoughts & Dialogue

So many thoughts distract our mind every minute. This internal dialogue and thoughts keep our mind occupied. Generally we do not notice these thoughts in our day-to-day life but while projecting when we require freeing our mind most from such thoughts we realise how difficult it is to get rid of such thoughts.

Silencing & Relaxing the Mind

- Keep focusing on your third eye.
- We can focus on our breathing rhythem.

- We can choose to use mantras, or simply count from 1 to 10 repeatedly.
- Just react like an observer of your thoughts but don't give heed to them. Don't try to analyze or react over them.
- We can simply focus on the blackness of our closed eyes or any imaginary dot.
- We need to narrow down our thoughts to a single string.
- We need to stop talking to our self and to listen – Listen to whatever sound we hear but not think about it. Simply listen to our thoughts without talking to our self and analyzing our thoughts. Different kind of sensations may occur, but they should be only registered as occurring, and we should not pay attention to them.
- Regular practice with these various techniques can help us to achieve a sound state of mind.

5. Misunderstanding Body Asleep vs. Relaxation

Beginners often get confused between Body Asleep and Relaxation. To project we need to learn how to fall asleep physically (i.e. body relaxation), but keep our consciousness away from slipping into a dream. We should stop feeling our physical body and rather concentrate on our consciousness.

6. The Visualization Problem

By visualizing our self out of body we try to exert pressure on our Astral body to exist. There may be many problems in visualization:

- While visualizing we have to actually see what we are visualizing but those people who lack imaginative power find it difficult to visualize.
- The greatest problem in visualization is we require imagining our self in a different position from the one we are in. Like, if we are lying down, we are in horizontal position but to exit we imagine us standing at the foot of the bed, which is vertical position. It consumes a lot of energy.

To overcome it we can follow these steps:

√ While lying down we must visualize our self floating above in air in same horizontal position.

√ Projecting by sitting in chair: While sitting on a chair we are in vertical position and we also visualize our self standing in front, in same vertical position (i.e. sitting and standing both are vertical positions).

7. Remembering the Projection

Many people encounter the problem of forgetting their Astral experiences.

I advise them to use following tips to remember their experiences:

♦ **Keep a Journal**

- The Astral experiences may seem so vivid and memorable when we wake up but they may erase from our memory even in a few minutes if we don't make a note of it. It is significant to record them.

♦ **Use Affirmations**

- We can use affirmations like: 'When I'll return, I'll remember all the experiences'. Such affirmations certainly have a positive impact.

- ♦ **Try Hard to Remember & Use Phrases**
- Try hard to remember the Astral experiences as soon as you wake up. Make it a regular habit to devote some time to think of Astral experiences.
- Use phrases in your mind to train your mind to remember:

  I was doing... I was meeting... I was seeing... I was travelling to... I was talking to... I was flying over... I was having a... I was at...

8. Paralysis, after an apparently Successful Projection

Sometimes we experience a weak projection or experience heavy exit sensations but not able to exit. Similarly, we feel sensations like heaviness, raised heart beats, vibrations etc. but we are not able to move and float our Astral body above. This is called waking paralysis.

This happens because we have activated our projection reflexes, and our etheric body has expanded but it has only partially freed from the astral body.

To overcome this we must:

- Put enough pressure on the astral body for separation.
- Increase the efforts of exit.
- Stop concentrating on these sensations and try to concentrate on exit.
- This Waking Paralysis can be converted into a lucid dream also. Concentrate on a fantasy place where you would like to go and whatever you wish to do there.

Astral Projection Tips

Before he left, I gave him a few suggestions that I hoped would help him to Astral travel:

1. Overcoming Fear

Our Astral body is invulnerable and can't be harmed in any way. We must have firm faith that Astral Projection is absolutely safe.

2. Practice Environment

Since Astral Projection requires to enter into a trance state, it is essential to create comfortable conditions and cut short the external disturbances:

Comfortable Room Temperature & Darkness:

- Practising at a comfortable temperature in a darkened room or wearing a sleeping mask promotes unobstructed exercise.
- The room should not be too cold or too hot, or too bright.
- Darken the room so that we don't see light through our eyelids.
- Those who fear darkness, should not turn off the all lights.

Noise Reduction

- Noise is one of the major distractions and reduction of such noises is compulsory for successful practice.
- Phone should be switched off and doors and windows should be closed.
- Those who live at a place where they face a lot of traffic and other sounds, they can use standard earmuffs or ear plugs.

- It is also preferable that no one is with the practitioner while practising.

Notify Others

- It's recommended to notify other inmates of your house not to disturb you.
- Some projectors have reported that they talk rapidly or nonsense during a projection and have rapid eye movements. This can make our loved ones worry about us.
- Pets should be kept out of the room and should be fed well before the performance of Astral techniques.

Remove Jewellery

- Before projecting we must remove all jewellery or other items that might be touching our skin. Our body might move erratically during projection which can cause us injury.
- Clothes can be removed or loose fitting clothes should be worn. We can cover our self a little extra to keep us slightly warmer than might generally be comfortable.

3. *Practise Regularly*

Astral Projection requires a lot of patience, determination and practice. To succeed in Astral Projection everyday practice is recommended.

4. *Approach to Literature*

We must obsess ourselves with the idea of Astral Projection for getting success because 'Intention is the key'. Literature is the main vehicle for disseminating information and impacts us deeply. We should read as much as we can about it and watch videos, movies and documentaries related to Astral Projection.

5. *Use an External Aid*

Astral Projection happens when the mind is able to achieve certain brain wave frequencies. External aid like binaural beats can be used to reach such frequencies. Binaural beats are musical recordings which helps the mind to reach the frequencies that make astral projection possible quicker and easier. These binaural beats can be easily downloaded from Internet.

6. *Remain Firmly Determined & Persistent*

Astral Projection may take a lot of time to occur. But it's worth waiting. For having a successful Astral experience it is essential to remain firmly determined. The intention and persistency are the keys to achieve success in Astral Projection.

7. *Proper Meditation*

For successful Astral Projection relaxation of mind and body is required. Only with a sound and silenced mind Astral Projection can be achieved. Proper meditation can help in calming and relaxing our mind.

8. *Manage Our Physical World*

Astral Projection needs sound mind. But if we are too stressed with our worries and our life is not manageable then we can't obtain relaxed feeling. So it is essential to manage our lives to get rid of unwanted tensions.

9. Be Aware & Open

You are required to increase your awareness level to be successful. You have to be open and aware and receptive for new experiences. With this increased receptivity and awareness, you could quickly open the doors to exotic and new experiences.

10. Communicating with Like-Minded People or Other Practitioners

Talking with like-minded people and successful practitioners can reduce our doubts and fears about Astral Projection. You can jointly project, or can take their help while projecting or can discuss personal experiences with other practitioners.

11. Personal Analysis

Every individual is unique and have different mental constitution than others. He may be having his own different kind of problems, whose solution probably can't be found in any book. Many things cannot be understood or described by others. The practitioners, who want to achieve excellent results, must focus on individual thought and form opinion based on personal independent analysis rather than finding every answer from books and other practitioners. This helps in advancing in Astral Projection. Practitioners should analyze personal successes and failures, and should apply a logical, even sceptical approach during research and practice.

12. Pen down Experiences

Writing your experiences is of great help in remembering and improving Astral Experiences. One should pen down all the experiences as soon as he wakes up. An effective journal should display a good number of indicators to help in statistical & comparative study to understand patterns.

It is recommended that every journal entry should include date, time and detailed experience. The problem faced during projection or mistakes committed and a plan of action for your next projection should also be written.

The Right Way to Maintain an Astral Travel Journal

The following sequence can be followed while writing an Astral travel journal:

1. Data:

a. Experience Serial Number

b. Date

c. Time

2. Detailed experience

3. Mistakes and problems faced

4. Plan of action for next projection

Miscellaneous Tips:

- Generate a sense of floating or sinking for you, but don't force exit. Then ask yourself, "How does it feel to be out of body?"
- When we do not get results right away we should not get too frustrated, stressed out; rather keep enjoying the Astral journey. There is a lot to learn down the way.
- We should not let doubt the reality and efficacy of Astral Projection because it is very real and everyone can do it.

- We can eat sugar-filled food or snack before projecting as it promotes more vivid projections.
- Like attracts like. So always practise in a good and positive mood. This will help in projecting to the higher Astral planes.
- We should avoid practising for more than 45 minutes at a stretch, otherwise we will be mentally exhausted.
- All the symptoms and sensations of Astral Projection are good signs. We should stay calm and not get panicked or get excited.
- Use of any kind of drugs or herbs to achieve a projection should be avoided.
- Lucid dreams can also be used as a gateway to Astral Projection.
- We must learn to focus. During Astral Projection concentration is very important.
- Astral Projection can help us in all areas of life. It can be used for problem solving.
- Progressive relaxation can be a very effective way to relax body and mind.
- After triggering separation we should move away from our body as soon as possible. The shorter the Silver Cord the more the attraction for physical body. Getting away from body prevents from snapping back into body.
- We must always pen down our Astral experiences.
- In case of suffering from Astral blindness, we must ask for eyes and move away from physical body.
- During Astral travel we should avoid invading the privacy of others.

- Intention and a strong desire with determination are keys to astral travel.
- We can protect our self by visualizing us surrounded by pure white bright light.
- We should remain positive and confident that we will be able to Astral travel and during Astral travel also we should remain positive and in a good mood and temperament.
- We must be prepared to allow OBE to happen. We should not panic when we feel OBE symptoms. We must learn to go with Astral symptoms and allow them to continue until we get free from physical body.
- Beginners should experiment with different methods and they must determine which method suits them best.
- Lie down with body along a north-south axis and the head pointed towards magnetic north.
- Use affirmations for lucid dreaming, projecting, not fearing and for remembering the Astral experiences. For example, affirmation like, "I'll have an outside-of-body experience everyday".

♦ ♦ ♦

Chapter 11

Frequently Asked Questions (FAQs)

Q.1. What is Astral Projection or Out-of-body experience?

Astral Projection or Out-of-body experience is a process through which our consciousness leaves our physical body and is free to travel anywhere, unrestricted by our normal physical boundaries.

We all unconsciously travel outside our bodies every night when we are asleep. But with the right guidance and practice, we can train ourselves to achieve this with 100% consciousness and awareness.

When we are born on this physical plane, we all come with a specific purpose. That purpose may be different for different people. But as we grow older, we forget why we are here. So we wander aimlessly and often end up wasting our lives.

Astral Projection is one way to help us know why we are here in the first place.

Q.2. Is there any perfect, easiest, infallible and fastest method of Astral Projection, which works for everyone?

Every individual is different from another. There is no single method which can be claimed to suit everybody. A technique which may work for your friend might not work on your personality. Everybody needs to explore the best method for himself by trial and error.

Q.3. Can everybody do the Astral Projection?

Yes, with instruction and guidance, almost everyone can have a Conscious Astral Projection.

Everyone experiences OBE at night when he/she sleeps. But since in sleep that kind of projection happens unconsciously, on waking up their astral experiences get distorted and they feel they have just had a dream.

Q.4. How often should we Project?

It is at our will, we can project as many times as we like. There is no harm in it. But as we have a life on this physical plane too, we need to maintain the balance between our astral and physical life.

Q.5. While Astral travelling, are we able to use our Senses? Can we See, Touch, Hear, Speak and Feel cold or heat, etc.?

While Astral travelling, we do not use our physical senses. But we can see, hear, and feel using our astral senses. We do not feel cold or hot in our astral body. If we feel them, that is because our physical body is feeling hot or cold, and that feeling is transferred to our Astral body through Silver Cord.

Q.6. Can Astral Projection be done without the supervision of any specialist. Can there be Harm in doing it?

Yes, Astral Projection can be done without the help of any specialist of this field. But without proper guidance and knowledge it may take a long time for us to project. That is why it is always advisable to get as much knowledge as possible in this field. Go through the related books time and again for reference and to strengthen your belief.

Fortunately there can't be any harm in doing astral projection. As I mentioned earlier we unconsciously are doing astral projection since our birth. But those who suffer any kind of mental disorders, it is not advisable for them to attempt Astral Projecting without consultation with their psychiatrist.

Q.7. How can we avoid being attached to our body when we go into trance?

In trance state our Astral body separates to physical body either wholly or partially. We need to have a strong will power and visualization exercises so that we can achieve a full separation.

Q.8. What is the best time to practise Astral Projection? Day, Night, or Early in the Morning?

There is no best time to practise. But for beginners I would recommend to practise during day time to avoid fear. But in day time we may face a lot of noise distraction, so I personally prefer early morning, when my mind and body both are in relaxed state.

Because of hectic lifestyle, most people prefer to practise at night, before going to sleep but they often end up falling asleep because their body is already too tired. For such people I recommend early morning time.

But there are as such no time boundaries for Astral Projection. It can be done any time according to convenience and when a person can relax.

Q.9. Should I practise lying down or sitting cross-legged?

Comfort must be the main deciding factor while choosing our practising position. But I prefer lying down position because it's more natural and distributes our weight equally.

We can choose any position we want to, as long as we are comfortable with that.

Q.10. How to connect with the spiritual self for Astral Project?

One need not be religious for doing Astral Projection. But one should have peace of mind during project. Keep negative thoughts away from mind, through Yoga practice, universal love and forgiveness, meditation and thought control. All these are of great importance.

Those who are religious can use religious prayers or chant mantras.

Some suggest becoming a vegan or a vegetarian.

Q.11. Can anyone Astral Project, irrespective of age?

Astral Projection has nothing to do with age. But the people suffering with serious psychological disorders, heart ailments or any major disease should avoid to project.

As we grow old we become more sceptic and fearful. Besides, children being more innocent, can learn it faster than adults, if given proper guidance.

Q.12. Once I am out of my body, how do I stay out?

For beginners generally it is not so easy to stay out of body for long. Their physical body needs their Astral body strongly. So initially they are not even accustomed to it. The fear of new world makes them enter into their body again. To stay out for long one should try to overcome his fear and move away from his physical body as much as and as soon as possible.

Q.13. Can Astral Projection be done whenever we want to?

Yes, Astral Projection can be done at any time, as far as the projector is able to relax his mind and it depends upon how experienced the Astral Projector is. Comfort and practice are the key factors.

Q.14. Can a Projector travel anywhere he wants to?

Yes, he can. There is no distance limit but for that one needs great proficiency and speed which comes with practice.

Strong control over thoughts and emotions is vital. A person can then visit outer space or planet too.

Q.15. How does it feel to be Out of Body?

That is really a wonderful experience. But it can't be explained here in words. Imagine you are free from physical restrictions and time limitations. There everything seems so real. There you can do what you can't do on physical plane. You can travel anywhere you wish to, meet other projectors, and meet even your loved departed ones, if they are on that plane.

To know exactly how great it feels during project, you must experience Astral Projection yourself.

Q.16. How can I be sure that I have projected and not imagined?

Astral Projection is like love and fragrance that can't be seen but perceived only. Initially projectors may get confused about its Reality or their Imagination. Once we experience it, we know it is absolutely real. Many advanced projectors have proved their projections as real by counter-verifying the knowledge they gained in astral plane.

Q.17. Sometimes our dreams are so vivid. Is this Astral Projection?

This might be a lucid dream or a real Astral Projection. Sometimes when we lose consciousness or fall asleep during Astral Projection then that projection takes the form of a lucid dream.

Q.18. Is Astral Projection something normal? Or is it unnatural and against God's will?

Astral Projection is perfectly normal. We all project during sleep. If it would have been against God's will then God would not have allowed this phenomenon. It rather confirms the belief in God and universal brotherhood.

Q.19. I have read a lot about Out-of-Body Experience, but I am not getting success. Why?

There might be several reasons. Please refer the chapter 'Astral Projection Problems and Mistakes'.

Q.20. Usually how long does it take?

That can't be said with certainty. Every person is different from another and has different belief system. Some people achieve their first OBE even at their first attempt and some try it for years. It varies from individual to individual.

Q.21. I visualize myself out of my Astral Body floating above? Is this the right technique?

Yes, this is a right technique.

Astral Projection requires more and more visualizations and the stronger the feelings and emotions, your astral body responds more and more.

Q.22. What kind of knowledge can we gain from the Astral Plane?

The Astral plane is a storehouse of unlimited and endless knowledge. We can know about our past, present, future and anything we want to. We can know about ancient civilizations and reach to other planets too. But we need to advance up to that level in projection.

Q.23. After Projection, when a person wakes up, does he/she feel fresh and revitalized, or feel exhausted?

Our physical body usually sleeps during Astral Projection, only our Astral body travels, so it doesn't exhaust the physical body.

Q.24. How long can we stay out of our body during Projection?

There is no time limitation for it. Usually beginners are not able to be out for a long time. One can project till the time his physical body allows him but when physical body wants your astral body back one has to go back and shouldn't try to resist. You know instinctively that it is time to Return.

Q.25. Can anyone get possessed during Projection?

This is a common fear and often most frequently asked question. Since our birth we are projecting unconsciously, have we ever got possessed till now?

No, we can't be possessed due to projection as our Astral body is attached to our physical body with a silver cord and no one can break that except at death.

Q.26. How to be sure that Astral Projection Experience was Real, Not an Imagination?

When we are in love, we can feel it and know its reality. Likewise once we achieve conscious OBE then we know that it is totally real, not an illusion or imagination.

Q.27. Which language is used in Astral Projection to communicate?

Normally, our own language, but actually it doesn't matter what language we speak, because communication is done telepathically in Astral.

Q.28. How accurately can you predict? How sure can you be of what you see? Is there a possibility of your seeing something wrong?

Sometimes it's very clear, and sometimes symbolic. In my case most of my dreams that are psychic are of a symbolic nature. I dreamt once that I was talking to my friend on phone who used to live in my city and telling her that I was missing her presence in my city. Two days later she was transferred to Delhi, yet I had not seen her transfer. I had only talked of missing her which was symbolic.

Q.29. Do dead people look same in appearance and can we touch them?

Dead people may have many appearances. If they have higher vibrations, they appear like a glowing star. They usually look younger than when they died and free of any physical flaws. They can also have various/unusual garments.

Yes, we may touch them, hug our loved departed ones in the Astral and it can be a very warming experience.

Q.30. Can we distinguish between a living person roaming in the Astral and a ghost?

Not always. Because we both are spirits without the body. We can ask the spirits if they have physical body or not.

Q.31. Can we see our past lives?

Yes, we can time-travel.

Once while projecting I expressed desire to see my past life, I saw myself a very beautiful Caucasian girl in my past life.

During OBE we can certainly explore past lives and old cultures.

Q.32. How to be sure that we had an Out-of-Body experience?

When we experience it fully and consciously we definitely know it.

Q.33. Whether Astral Projection is safe or not?

This is the most common fear which deters people from projecting. But we must agree that during sleep we all project unconsciously. Astral Projection is just a natural experience reported in every civilization of the world. It is safe for most of the people. But people who have any acute psychological problems should avoid it.

Q.34. Can Astral Projection lead to oversleep. How to keep a track on time?

Our bodies have an inner biological clock, and it calls our Astral body back when the time arrives. So it is almost impossible to oversleep.

Q.35. Sometimes Out-of-Body Experiences happen without any practice, but such unconscious OBE's seem to lack any direction, and it becomes very tough to have control over them. What should one do?

In such situation one should practise more for conscious Astral Projection to gain control over Astral experiences.

Q.36. Is it possible to be out of body and at the same time feel the sleeping physical body?

Yes, it is called "dual-consciousness".

In dual consciousness we can feel both Physical and Astral body. We can see and feel our physical body lying down and we can move our Astral body at the same time.

Q.37. Is Astral Projection scientifically proved?

Earlier science didn't pay attention to Astral Projection. But from past half a century this concept has taken scientific approach.

Muldoon and Carrington did the first main study in 1951 by collecting and studying over 100 cases of Astral Projection.

The father of NDEs (Near Death Experiences), Raymond

A. Moody through his very popular book 'Life after Life' and by his scientific research has made a noteworthy contribution in reinforcing scientific beliefs in Astral Projection.

Q.38. How can Astral Projection help our physical body, mind and soul?

Astral Projection heals our mind, body, soul and calms our mind and relaxes our body. It helps in spiritual advancement and induces the feeling of universal brotherhood. We come to know the purpose of our life.

Q.39. Does Astral activity have any Karmic consequences?

Yes, there is Karmic consequence of whatever we do. Whatever wrong we do with our physical as well as Astral body we are responsible and answerable for it.

Q.40. Can Astral Projection help us to see and meet God?

Can we see the love or smell? No, because they are not tangible. Likewise God is also intangible. Seeing God is like seeing love or smell. But like love and smell, God can also be experienced and felt. Astral Projection can help us to experience God if we really want that.

Q.41. Can Astral Projection help us to travel thousands or millions of light years away in an instant to go to outer space and other planets?

Yes, it helps.

Unlike our physical body there is no limit for Astral body. Our Astral body can move with amazing speed. But experience is required to master control over speed and thoughts.

Q.42. How much common this Astral Projection concept is?

Study shows that Astral Projection is experienced, probably by 5% to 10% of the world's population.

Q.43. Can Astral Projection change a person's religious beliefs?

Study shows that Astral Projection experiences do not change one's religious beliefs. It rather confirms our religious beliefs and such people become more spiritual.

Q.44. Can any experienced Astral Projector help others in Astral Travel?

Yes, if the other person calls or invites for help. But it may not be a good thing to do at all the times.

Q.45. Can Astral Projection be proved real?

Like love, god and smell it is something to be felt. It is very difficult to prove it to another person. The person who has Astral experience definitely believes in it and remains 100% sure about it. If someone wants to know whether it's real or not then he himself should try and know it. No proof can be better than self experience.

Q.46. Can we take objects back from Astral Travelling?

We can't take back any objects because they are on other energy level in Astral. We can take back experiences, information and intelligence, but not objects.

Q.47. How to make Astral Experience last longer? Is there time limit or how long can anyone stay out of body?

Experienced projectors can stay out for several hours and newbies for a few minutes. Though we cannot stay out for years because we have a life on earth and we have to wake up in our physical body. It is advised not to stay out when our physical body wants us back.

Q.48. Is it possible to stay in the Astral Plane forever and not come back?

No, it's possible only after death, when the silver cord is broken. Our experiences in the Astral Plane deepen our understanding and awareness and love for life. After Astral Travel we come back more spiritually advanced. Astral experiences make us realize that life on earth has a purpose. So willingly, we won't be trying to escape into the Astral.

Though we can stay in the Astral Plane for an indefinite period when we are dead, our spirit heals and then we come back and take new bodies i.e. rebirth.

Q.49. Can we enter another person's dreams during projection?

We cannot control someone else's incidents, experiences, views and dreams.

Though we can become part of someone's dreams or Astral experiences when we are out of our physical body just as we can be part of someone's life when we are inside our physical body.

Q.50. Is there possibility that two or more people in one room or living away do Astral Projection at the same time and then be able to see and meet each other in Astral?

Yes, we can Astral Project jointly, see and meet each other in Astral, and share an Astral experience.

Q.51. Do Astral Entities Really Exist? Are they Aangerous, and can hurt or harm? How to avoid such negative Astral entities and protect ourselves from them?

Yes, Astral entities exist. We are not the only creatures in Astral world.

First thing is we should avoid calling and inviting unknown spirits. These Astral entities can't harm us, unless we permit them to frighten us. Keep away from their thinking and being afraid of them. They can terrorize us only if we are scared of them. They can't hurt us. Be happy, bright, and optimistic because negative entities dislike that. So they will stay away from us. They approach us only if they realize that we are weak and scared of them and have negative vibes.

We can also use some Astral Self-Defence Techniques by surrounding our self with bright white light to keep bad entities away.

Q.52. What should one do and how should one react, when he encounters any bad Astral entity?

The best thing we can do in this condition is to remain calm and not feel afraid or panic. The negative entity will itself leave us then. Alternatively, we can use a psychic self-defence technique, request our spirit guide or deity we worship for help, or can ask for wearing a protective amulet to ward off negative entities.

Q.53. How to return to physical body? Is there possibility to stay out?

The actual difficulty is about getting out of the body. Not of getting in.

When the time comes for return our body calls itself or if you wish to go back then just think of getting into your body and the next moment you will find yourself back into your body.

Q.54. Is there any fast, unfailing, consistent method of Astral Projection, which guarantees 100% surety of Astral Projection?

Unfortunately there is no such method. Every individual has to strive to find his reliable method himself. Everyone is unique; the technique which may be working for your friend might not work for you. So one has to try with many of these techniques and choose the one that suits him best.

♦♦♦

BOOKS ON ASTRAL

ISBN: 978-81-7806-064-4

₹96/-

ISBN: 978-81-7806-401-7

₹395/-

ISBN: 978-81-7806-108-5

₹125/-

ISBN: 978-81-7806-136-8

₹125/-

ISBN: 978-81-7806-143-6

₹250/-

ISBN: 978-81-7806-117-7

₹110/-

UNICORN BOOKS

Also available online at:

www.unicornbooks.in • www.filpkart.com • www.snapdeal.com • www.ebay.in